LAW BASICS

Student Study Guides

SUCCESSION

FOURTH EDITION

LAW
BASICS
Student Study Guides

SUCCESSION

FOURTH EDITION

By

Alex Gibb, LLB (Hons)
Lecturer in Law, North East Scotland College

and

Alasdair Bothwell Gordon, LLB, BD (Hons), EdD, TQFE, LCGI
Former Lecturer in Law, North East Scotland College

W. GREEN

THOMSON REUTERS

First Edition published in 1999
Second Edition published in 2007
Third Edition published in 2012
Fourth Edition published in 2018

ISBN 978-0-414-06514-7

Published in 2018 by Thomson Reuters,
trading as W. Green, 21 Alva Street, Edinburgh, EH2 4PS.
thomson reuters is registered in England & Wales, Company No.1679046.
registered Office and address for service: 5 Canada Square, Canary Wharf, London, E14 5AQ.
For further information on our products and services, visit http://www.sweetandmaxwell.co.uk/wgreen

Computerset by W. Green
Printed and bound by CPI Group (UK) Ltd, Croydon, CR0 4YY

No natural forests were destroyed to make this product:
only farmed timber was used and replanted.

A CIP catalogue record of this book is available from the British Library.

Orders by email to: TRLUKI.orders@thomsonreuters.com
General enquiries should be directed to: wgreen.enquiries@thomson.com

ABOUT THE AUTHORS

Alex Gibb is a Lecturer in Law at North East Scotland College. *Succession Law*Basics is the second of Alasdair Gordon's titles he has updated, following *Contract Law*Basics, which is likewise now in its 4th Edition. Mr Gibb is also a contributing author to the student textbooks *Understanding Scots Law* and *Business Law in Scotland.*

Dr Alasdair Gordon is a former Lecturer in Law at Aberdeen College (now North East Scotland College). During his distinguished career in education Dr Gordon has helped countless students, both through his many years of teaching and through his numerous written works.

FOREWORD

It was a pleasure and a privilege, some years ago, to be invited by Greens to write two of the earlier volumes in the *Law*Basics Series, on *Contract Law* and on *Succession*, which were published in 1998 and 1999 respectively. Both of these books went on to second editions under my authorship. The *Law*Basics textbooks are now almost at the end of their third decade and their continued popularity speaks for itself.

When I wrote the original volumes, I was a lecturer at Aberdeen College, now part of North East Scotland College. I am now retired and have been away from teaching for a number of years. It is a particular pleasure to me that the authorship of subsequent editions, both of *Contract Law* and *Succession*, has been undertaken by Alex Gibb, also a lecturer at North East Scotland College. Mr Gibb has skilfully adapted, updated, improved and clarified these texts.

I am very pleased to commend Mr Gibb's fourth edition of *Succession* *Law*Basics to today's students in the expectation it will be as well received as the earlier editions and will continue to be a good and useful foundation for their studies in Scots Law.

Alasdair B. Gordon
Hamilton, South Lanarkshire
June 2018

PREFACE

The law of succession affects us all. Virtually everyone owns property, and absolutely everyone dies. The issue of what should be done with our property when we die lies at the heart of succession law. A basic working knowledge of the legal rules regulating succession is potentially useful to everyone, especially those who wish to make provision for the distribution of their own property after death.

In the tradition of the *Law*Basics series, it is the aim of this modest book to provide the reader with a solid foundation in the Scots law of succession. It is written primarily for students, whom it is hoped will find it useful both as a learning resource and revision aid, but the approachable style might also make the text of interest to the general reader. It should be noted that whilst gender-neutral terminology has been employed where possible, at times masculine terms have been used purely in the interests of word economy. The intention, however, is to be inclusive, so "he" can be read as "he or she" and "his" includes "his or her" unless the context clearly indicates otherwise.

Succession is an area of the law which undergoes fairly regular changes. The first edition of this book was published in 1999 under the authorship of Alasdair Gordon, who also produced a second edition in 2007. I was honoured to be entrusted with the task of updating Dr Gordon's excellent work in the form of a third edition in 2012, and I remain immensely proud to now be producing this fourth edition of the book. It has always been my intention to retain the spirit and maintain the high quality of Dr Gordon's text, whilst making certain necessary updates and humbly introducing my own stylistic alterations. Striking such a balance is no easy task, and I consider it a compliment of the highest order that, once again, the finished work has been commended by Dr Gordon himself; I can only hope that the book is as well received by its readers.

My aim has been to state the law as at 31 March 2018. Responsibility for any errors or omissions is mine alone.

Alex Gibb
Aberdeen, June 2018

CONTENTS

TABLE OF CASES

1. INTRODUCTION TO THE LAW OF SUCCESSION

Succession is the area of law that regulates the passing of a person's property after his or her death. Even a person of the most modest means will leave behind a certain amount of property, and it is only logical that something must be done with these belongings. Sometimes, the value of the property that a deceased has left behind will be very high and sometimes it will be very low; most often, the value falls somewhere in the middle of these two extremes. Regardless of the sums involved, the principles behind the law of succession remain the same; to determine who has the right to take ownership of the deceased's property and to calculate exactly what these entitlements amount to. **1–01**

HISTORICAL BACKGROUND

Every legal system acknowledges some form of the law of succession. Ever since civilisations developed to the point where there was respect for the personal ownership of property, there has been the question of who should get what when a person dies. In most modern democratic legal systems, the law has had to maintain a balance between giving effect to the wishes of the deceased and treating the survivors (particularly close family members) in a fair and equitable manner. **1–02**

The historical emphasis of succession was the continuation of the family line and, to this end, identification of an "heir" (person entitled to inherit) was of paramount importance. Due to the patriarchal nature of traditional Western societies, males would always be favoured over females, and the first-born son would often inherit the majority of his deceased father's "estate" (property left behind upon death). The claims of female family members were secondary to this and more commonly involved occupation rights than a right to actually take ownership of property.

Of course, in modern times such gender inequality is viewed as entirely unacceptable, and significant steps have been taken in many areas of the law towards ensuring parity of treatment between the sexes. Discussion of whether or not such advancements have created the desired equality is far beyond the scope of this book, but what can certainly be said is that the rules of succession in Scotland nowadays make no distinction between males and females in terms of inheriting property.

SUCCESSION IN MODERN TIMES

With the fading importance of identifying a single heir to one's estate, succession is now more concerned with the distribution of property among the deceased person's beneficiaries, of which there may be any number. Broadly speaking, the rules of succession are divided into two distinct **1–03** areas; those that regulate the situation where the deceased left no will (called "intestate succession") and those that regulate the situation where the deceased did leave a will (called "testate succession"). Both of these areas present their own specific challenges to the legal practitioner, from the rigid and generalised rules of intestate succession, to the sometimes surprising (and often unpalatable) provisions that are contained in some wills. It is probably, on balance, the preferable situation where the deceased has left at least some indication of what he wished done with his property, though in reality it is still a minority of the population who actually leave any precise instructions by will as to the disposal of their estate.

There can be little doubt that, whether distribution of an estate is to be affected according to the rules of testacy or intestacy, close family members occupy the most favourable positions in terms of inheritance. Although there is no longer any preference between male and female heirs, the position of children is still a very powerful one. Further direct descendants of the deceased (known collectively with any children as "issue") have also been given greater recognition. The position of spouse (or, more recently, civil partner) is also much stronger now than in previous times, particularly in terms of intestate division. In-roads have also been made into recognising the rights of cohabiting partners.

The intention behind many rules of succession is to achieve a fair balance between these competing interests. It must be said, however, that succession is an area of law that can be very divisive among members of a family, where perceptions of what is "fair" are often clouded by what one actually stands to inherit.

PROPERTY, SUCCESSION AND TRUSTS

1–04 Property is of paramount significance to the law of succession. It is important at the outset to understand the basic principle of Scots law that, broadly speaking, property can be divided into two categories; heritable and moveable. Heritable property is classed as land and anything attached to the land such as buildings and naturally growing crops. Moveable property is anything that cannot be classed as heritable and so includes a multitude of items, though perhaps for succession purposes money would be the most important example. This may seem simple enough, but there are a good number of fine distinctions between the two classifications, which will be considered in more detail in Ch.2.

Regardless of whether the deceased leaves behind heritable or moveable property (very commonly the estate comprises a mixture of both), it is a practical reality of succession that someone is required to take responsibility of this property on behalf of the deceased and administer the process of its transfer to the appropriate beneficiaries. This person is called the "executor", and it is his role to ensure that the deceased's property is fully ingathered after death and distributed correctly according to the relevant rules of division (testacy or intestacy as applicable). The executor therefore takes control of the deceased's property and will often retain it in his possession whilst the rights of the beneficiaries are determined. However, it is important to note that the executor does not own this property free of obligations and has rights over it only as are necessary for the carrying out of his duties. The executor is said to hold the property "in trust" for the benefit of the deceased's survivors, and there is therefore a strong link between the law of succession and the law of trusts (i.e. the area of law regulating property that is held and administered by one person for the benefit of another). Further coverage on trusts will be provided in Ch.11, and the role of the executor itself will be fully considered in Ch.10.

THE LEGAL BASIS OF SUCCESSION

As with many other areas of law in Scotland, succession has been **1–05** developed largely through common law and has never been fully codified. That said, the area was radically overhauled by the Succession (Scotland) Act 1964 ("the 1964 Act"), a statute which, among other things, introduced significant rights for surviving spouses upon intestacy. Since its passing, the 1964 Act has been regularly amended and updated, commonly for practical purposes such as increasing certain financial limits to correspond with inflationary rises. The general statutory regime has also been altered by various pieces of separate legislation, such as the Civil Partnership Act 2004 and the Family Law (Scotland) Act 2006. More recently, the Succession (Scotland) Act 2016 ("the 2016 Act") effected further reform, largely regarding practical aspects of the area. The 2016 Act implemented various recommendations made by the Scottish Law Commission in its extensive *Report on Succession* (HMSO, 2009), Scot. Law Com. No.215, although many aspects reported on were left unchanged. The Scottish Government has indicated that further reform is still to come, but at the time of writing the shape which this might take remains to be seen.

PRIVATE INTERNATIONAL LAW

Scotland's succession laws are distinct from that of any other country, and **1–06** whilst assistance on certain matters has at times been sought from other jurisdictions, there is no legal system whose regime in this area is entirely comparable. Of particular note is the fact that, despite Scotland's long-standing constitutional union with England and the resulting similarities in many guiding principles and opinions, the rules of succession between the two countries are in many respects quite different.

This diversity of approaches can occasionally lead to problems where two legal systems claim jurisdiction over the same estate. This is particularly relevant in the UK, where it is very possible for the same individual to have property interests in both Scotland and England. Indeed, it is also possible (though rarer) for property interests to extend beyond the boundaries of the UK, or for a foreign national to have property interests in Scotland whilst being permanently based abroad. Such issues are dealt with under private international law, which is an area of legal expertise in its own right; as a result, only brief commentary can be made in a book of this size.

There are two general rules as developed by Scottish common law. The first is that the Scots law of succession applies to moveable property owned by any person who is "domiciled" in Scotland. Domicile is a difficult term to define; it is distinct from residence, which can be a more transient concept, and it is different also from place of birth which, although fixed, need not have much significance to a person's current circumstances. Domicile is perhaps best taken to mean the place where a person makes his permanent home. Therefore, regardless of where moveable property is located at any particular time, if it is owned by a person domiciled in Scotland, the Scots law rules of succession apply to it. The second rule is that any "immoveable" property situated in Scotland is also subject to the Scottish laws, regardless of where the owner is domiciled. The term "immoveable" is not exactly the same as heritable, since the latter is broader, but for practical purposes means something very similar, i.e. land and buildings.

2. PRACTICAL MATTERS UPON DEATH

Succession only operates when someone has died. This may sound obvious in the extreme, but it is actually a very important issue that can give rise to a number of problems. The exact moment of death can sometimes be difficult (or even impossible) to identify, which leaves the law of succession struggling somewhat to regulate the passing of the deceased's property. There are also potential problems when two or more people die at or around the same time, especially if they are the beneficiaries of each others' estates. Even in the absence of such complications, death obliges a number of practical matters to be dealt with. **2–01**

THE FACT OF DEATH

In the vast majority of cases, the fact as well as the date and time of a person's death can be determined without difficulty. Modern science and medicine have, in some ways, made the concept of death less precise and Scots law, like most legal systems, is still coming to terms with the distinction between physical death and brain death. Many people attempt to provide for difficult situations by executing what is misleadingly called a "living will", i.e. a statement of how they wish to be treated in the event of life threatening illness or trauma. This is a complex area far beyond the scope of this book, and it is sufficient to say that a "living will" is not a testamentary document and is therefore not relevant to succession. **2–02**

Before an estate can be administered, death must be established and would have to be proved in the rare event of a challenge. Normal practice is for a doctor to issue a medical certificate confirming the time, place and cause of the death. The death must then be registered with the Registrar of Births, Marriages and Deaths within eight days. An extract from the Register of Deaths is regarded as sufficient (but not conclusive) evidence of death under s.41(3) of the Registration of Births, Marriages and Deaths (Scotland) Act 1965.

However, a doctor can only issue a death certificate after viewing identified human remains. Problems obviously arise where there are no such remains.

PRESUMPTION OF DEATH

Under Scottish common law, if a person disappeared, there was no presumption other than that his life continued to the extremes of old age. In *Secretary of State for Scotland v Sutherland*, 1944 S.C. 79, a husband had disappeared and had not been heard of for 42 years. The wife applied for a declarator that he was now dead. The court adhered to the presumption that he was still alive, now aged 72. Anyone trying to overturn the common **2–03** law presumption also required proof beyond reasonable doubt, a much higher standard than normally required in a civil case. In the earlier case of *Greig v Merchant Company of Edinburgh*, 1921 S.C. 76, a husband had been absent for 10 years. There was good medical evidence that his alcoholic lifestyle would have killed him before then. The court accepted that he was dead and his widow was thus able to claim her pension.

Clearly, the common law was somewhat rigid in this area and could cause considerable distress. There are now statutory presumptions under the Presumption of Death (Scotland) Act 1977 ("the 1977 Act"). Under this Act, anyone having an interest to do so may raise an action to have a person declared legally dead. This applies in two main circumstances:

(1) Where someone is thought to have died at or around a particular time. An example would be where an air accident occurred over the ocean and no human remains could be recovered.

(2) Where someone has not been known to be alive for a period of at least seven years. To put it another way, the person simply disappears. With modern forms of communication it is much more difficult for a living person to disappear, but it is still possible.

Proof of death under the 1977 Act is on a balance of probabilities, as would be normal in civil cases. If it cannot be proved exactly when death took place, but that it must have been between date A and date B, B will be the date of death as per the court decree. If the deceased has simply disappeared, death will be deemed to have taken place at the end of the day seven years after he was last known to be alive.

The decree allows the executor to proceed with the administration of the estate. Insurance companies need not allow payment of a life policy proceeds purely on the evidence of a declarator of death although, in practice, most do. Any marriage (or civil partnership) of the deceased is dissolved.

Though unlikely, it is possible for the "deceased" to reappear. This does not revive a marriage or civil partnership, although any pre-decree criminal liability is revived. The person must apply for a recall of the declarator of death and may also be able to reclaim such value of distributed property as is deemed "fair and reasonable". In practice, the executor will often take out an insurance policy to safeguard against this situation.

SURVIVORSHIP

2–04 Before a beneficiary can inherit, it must be shown that he survived the deceased. This is usually unproblematic, but complications can occur in cases of "common calamity" where more than one person is killed in the same incident. An easy example is a car crash. If, as is often the case, the parties are related or are close friends, the question of inheritance may arise.

Where it can actually be proved that one party survived the other, even by seconds, then rights may pass from one estate to the other. Proof only requires the normal civil standard of balance of probability. Suppose John and Jean are both killed in a common calamity. John has made a will leaving everything to Jean. If John dies first, his estate vests in Jean and there is no minimum period of time required for her survivorship. John's estate forms part of her estate and will be divided among her heirs. However, if Jean dies before John, she acquires no vested right and John's estate will be divided according to the rules of intestate succession (unless the will has made alternative provisions).

If there is no proof, certain presumptions will be used. Under common law, there was no presumption and both parties were presumed to have died at exactly the same time. This meant that there could be no passing of property from one estate to the other, which occasionally led to unsatisfactory results. In *Drummond's Judicial Factor v HM Advocate*, 1944 S.C. 298, a husband and wife both died, intestate, during a bomb blast. The husband had surviving siblings, but the wife had no surviving relatives. If the husband was deemed to have survived his wife, both his and his wife's estate could have been claimed by his surviviors. However, in absence of any evidence regarding survivorship, the court rejected this claim and the wife's estate passed to the Crown as final heir. In *Ross's Judicial Factor v Martin*, 1955 S.C. (HL) 56, two sisters had "mirror-image" wills leaving everything to the other, "whom failing" a named charity, i.e. if the other had died first the charity would inherit. They both died as a result of a gas leak and there was no indication as to which had died first. Because, at common law, neither had survived the other, the "whom failing" clauses could not operate. Both of their estates had to be divided according to intestate succession, which meant that the charity had no claim. Clearly this interpretation did not achieve the result the sisters would have wished.

The severity of the common law gave way to somewhat kinder presumptions under statute. The 1964 Act began the legislative reform by providing that where survivorship cannot be proven in a common calamity, the general rule is that the younger person is presumed to have survived the elder. This was subject to two important exceptions:

(1) Where the parties were spouses or civil partners, the presumption was that they died simultaneously and that neither survived the other. In effect, this meant that their estates were divided as though they had been single people.

(2) If the older person had made a bequest in favour of the younger person, whom failing a third party *and* the younger person was intestate, the older party, for the purpose of that bequest only, was presumed to have survived the younger. (This seems complicated, but the effect was simply to allow the third party to inherit.)

However, the 2016 Act introduced significant changes in this area by removing the basic presumption of younger surviving elder. Instead, where order of death is uncertain, each deceased is treated as having failed to survive the other. Further, a "whom failing" clause will apply regardless of whether the first-named beneficiary was intestate or not. This appears in many ways to be a reversion to the common law position, with new provisions addressing the problem encountered in the *Ross* case. However, the *Drummond* problem would still not be remedied under the statutory provisions.

Perhaps the best conclusion to draw is that, as with many areas, having a valid will in place is the best way to avoid survivorship problems. In practice, many wills provide that a beneficiary must survive the testator for a certain period, often 30 days, which further helps to reduce complications.

THE UNWORTHY HEIR

2–05 There may be certain circumstances in which someone is debarred from inheriting by virtue of his conduct. The rule in Scots law preventing an unworthy heir inheriting appears derives from both statute and common law, although for a long time the only cases in point were English. In Scotland, the matter was first considered judicially in the sheriff court case of *Smith, Petitioner*, 1979 S.L.T. (Sh. Ct) 35, in which it was held that there was an absolute bar on inheriting if there was a conviction against the heir for murder or culpable homicide.

An old statute, the Parricide Act 1594, dealt with the killing of parents and grandparents, but its scope was never entirely clear and applying it was very difficult. It was eventually abolished under s.17 of the 2016 Act, but it had long been obsolete in a practical sense. Statutory reform began by way of the Forfeiture Act 1982, which gave the court power, at its discretion, to modify the extent of the forfeiture in the case of "unlawful killing", but not murder. In Scotland, this would mean that forfeiture could, but need not be, modified in the case of culpable homicide. In *Gilchrist, Petitioner*, 1990 S.L.T. 494, a wife who had killed her husband after suffering emotional abuse was convicted of culpable homicide and admonished. The wife raised a petition seeking an order under the Act, modifying the common law rule by which she could not benefit from her own crime. It was held that, in all the circumstances of the case, an order modifying the rule in respect of 80 per cent of the estate was appropriate.

Under s.12 of the 2016 Act, a person barred from inheriting is treated as having failed to survive the deceased. A further reform enacted by the 2016 Act is that the court now has power to exclude the forfeiture rule entirely, if appropriate in the circumstances. This was not previously possible; in *Cross, Petitioner*, 1987 S.L.T. 384, it had been observed that the court did not have power to exclude the rule entirely, but it was held that in those circumstances that the forfeiture should be modified to 99 per cent of the estate.

DEBTS

2–06 An oft-asked question in the area of succession is, do a deceased's debts die with him? The answer to this is not entirely straightforward, partly because the legal existence of a debt and the fact of that debt actually being paid are not always the same thing and also because death itself creates debts of various types. There are, however, a number of important points to note which, when taken together, will make the full situation clear.

First, it can be stated without doubt that the vast majority of existing debts accrued during a person's lifetime do not simply "disappear" upon death. Instead, they become debts liable to be paid out of the deceased's estate. (An exception to this is student loans, which will usually be cancelled if they remain unpaid upon the borrower's death.) Secondly, the administration of the deceased's estate will create a number of "new" debts, such as the expenses of the executor and certain other claims. Thirdly, all debts must be applied to the estate in accordance with a pre-determined "rank" outlined by statute. The value of the estate that remains after all debts have been settled then passes on to the beneficiaries by function of inheritance. If the total estate is exhausted by the payment of outstanding debts, any remaining debts are written off; they do not pass on to be paid by the deceased's descendants.

A further point worth noting is that many people make arrangements for certain debts to be paid upon their death. For example, many homeowners who are required to repay a secured loan on their house will also take out a life assurance policy with sufficient proceeds to cover the outstanding balance of the secured loan. Upon death, the insurance policy effectively negates this particular debt, although the mechanism by which this occurs may be somewhat more complicated than that. This issue is considered further below, and certain other matters relating to executry practice are considered in Ch.10. For now, it is sufficient to understand that the deceased's debts must be paid before his estate can be divided among the beneficiaries.

INHERITANCE TAX

It has been said that there are only two certainties in life; death and taxes. **2–07**
True or false, the two can certainly be connected. Since the 17th century, successive governments have realised that death can be a convenient time to tax a person's estate. Originally, "death duty" would be calculated on what the deceased owned at the time of death. An obvious form of avoidance would be for an older person to pass on at least some of his property to his heirs before death. The rules of taxation were then extended to include property thus transferred for a limited period before death. For most of the 20th century, the main tax payable upon death was called estate duty, replaced briefly by capital transfer tax. In 1986, this was replaced by inheritance tax ("IHT").

IHT, like most taxation, is complex and continually liable to change. Accordingly, only very general comments can be made in a book of this size and, even then, with the caveat that governments can—and do—change their minds.

The Ineritance Tax Act 1984 provides that IHT is charged on the loss of value caused to an estate when a transfer is made, unless it is an exempt transfer. Death counts as a transfer of the entire estate. If a transfer is made more than seven years before death, it is exempt and no IHT is paid on that property. Thus if Albert gives his son Brian £100,000 and dies ten years thereafter, no tax is payable on that sum. But, if Albert dies within seven years, IHT is payable, although it may be reduced by "taper relief" depending on when, within that period, the transfer was made. Transfers between spouses or civil partners during lifetime or as a result of succession are totally exempt from IHT. Other major exemptions are donations to registered UK charities and for certain gifts and reasonable maintenance of relatives. There is also an additional measure currently being phased in allowing a family residence to be passed on to direct descendants free of IHT.

The basis of valuation of estates is outlined in Ch.10 and IHT is charged on the value of the net estate, i.e. after deduction of allowable debts and funeral expenses. At the time of writing, the first £325,000 of an estate is exempt from IHT (or, more precisely, is taxed at a nil rate) and thereafter the rate is 40 per cent. Thus, if a total net estate is £340,000, only £15,000 is liable to be taxed at 40 per cent, so the amount charged would be £6,000. It is also worth noting that other rules exist which may impact upon this threshold; for example, in October 2007, a mechanism was introduced to allow any unused IHT exemption from a deceased's estate to be transferred to a surviving spouse or civil partner, effectively increasing the survivor's threshold to (potentially) £650,000.

In practice, only a small minority of all estates in Scotland are actually liable to IHT. However, any testator whose estate might potentially attract an IHT liability is strongly advised to obtain professional advice.

THE DECEASED'S PROPERTY

2–08 In most cases, the deceased's estate is not exhausted by outstanding debts. (Indeed, if this were not so, succession law would be largely pointless!) It is very important, therefore, to consider at this point certain rules that apply to the remaining estate. In Ch.1, the broad distinction between heritable and moveable property was outlined. This distinction can be very important, particularly regarding the issue of legal rights, which are only claimable on the moveable estate.

In essence, the distinction between heritable and moveable is simple. Heritable property refers to land and to items permanently attached to it, such as buildings, houses, walls and trees growing in the ground. All property that is not heritable is counted as moveable. Property law also distinguishes between corporeal and incorporeal items, which can be either heritable or moveable. If property is corporeal it has a physical existence and the five senses can, at least in theory, be applied to it. Corporeal property could include land, houses, cars and furnishings. Incorporeal property is invisible and could include items such as a lease, shares in a company and a very wide variety of rights. The distinction between corporeal and incorporeal property has little direct relevance to the law of succession.

In the majority of cases, it is easy to know into which category any given property falls. Most property is obviously either heritable or moveable by nature. There can occasionally be problems. There is, in the law of succession, a particular legal fiction that allows certain moveable property to be "constructively" converted into heritage. Thus, money required for the completion of an unfinished building counts as heritage and heirs would not be able to claim legal rights out of it. In the old case of *Johnston v Dobie* (1783) Mor. 5443, it was held that building materials piled on the ground beside an incomplete structure counted as heritable property.

A particular problem can arise in the case of goodwill of a business. Goodwill is an elusive concept at the best of times, yet anyone buying or selling a business is well aware that it can be a valuable asset. In fact, goodwill may be heritable or moveable or a mixture of the two. If the business is closely associated with particular premises, such as a well-known and established hotel, the goodwill will generally count as heritable. If the reputation of the business relied mainly on the deceased's skill and personal reputation, the goodwill will be moveable. Obviously, there are times where the goodwill will be a mixture of the two and a precise apportionment between heritable and moveable may well be problematic. A related rule regarding businesses can be found under s.22 of the Partnership Act 1890, which states that a partner's share in a firm's assets count as moveable, even if some or all of these assets are actually heritable, such as a farming partnership.

Another potential problem area is that of fixtures, i.e. items that were moveable but have become part of the heritage. Suppose Jake buys an antique mantelpiece and has it built into his living room. At the same time, he has a new fitted carpet laid. He dies, leaving a will providing that his house, i.e. heritage, goes to Robert and the contents, i.e. moveables, goes to Freda. How does one categorise the mantelpiece and the fitted carpet? Unless the will expressly deals with the matter, the presumptions of the so-called law of fixtures apply. The presumption would be that the mantelpiece is permanently attached to the property, and the courts have tended to favour the person entitled to succeed to the heritage, so that he takes it in the same condition in which the deceased enjoyed it. However, the fitted carpet would likely not count as a permanent attachment and therefore would be a moveable asset.

If the deceased had agreed to sell heritable property but, at the time of death, the transaction had not been settled, the heritage would count as a heritable asset with a nil value but the amount of the price unpaid would be a moveable asset, as would any sum already paid to account. If the deceased had, conversely, agreed to buy heritable property but had not paid for it, that property would count as a heritable asset and the unpaid price would be a moveable debt.

If the deceased's heritable property was mortgaged, i.e. subject to a standard security, the debt, or loan outstanding, counts as heritable and is deducted from the value of the heritage. If the deceased was a creditor in a standard security over another person's property, the value of the security counts as moveable but not in respect of legal rights or taxation, where it counts as heritable (this simply means that legal rights cannot be claimed out of the value of the standard security). The word "mortgage" is used popularly to describe a loan advanced to a buyer of heritable property, though strictly speaking this term is inaccurate; however, it is used here for reasons of convenience.

Many people who have received a loan secured over their property will have some form of mortgage protection policy to pay off the outstanding capital sum in the event of death. It is important to notice that the secured loan is a heritable debt and the proceeds of the policy count as a moveable asset. The debt is not automatically extinguished.

If the loan is an endowment mortgage, the debtor pays interest only but, in addition, pays premiums on an endowment insurance policy which, at the end of its term or on the earlier death of the insured, will produce (in theory) at least an adequate sum to repay the original amount borrowed. In a traditional endowment mortgage, the debt is doubly secured. There will be a standard security over the heritable property and the insurance policy will have been assigned to the lender and that assignation duly intimated to the insurance company. In such a case, the debt would be deducted from heritable and moveable estate in proportion to the respective values of the heritage and the policy. If the policy has not been properly assigned to the lender, the debt is not doubly secured and all the proceeds simply count as a moveable asset.

It can probably be deduced from the above that this is another potentially complicated area, taking in fields of legal study that are beyond the scope of this book. To reiterate earlier advice, anyone whose estate might be affected by such complexities is advised to obtain professional advice.

3. INTESTATE SUCCESSION

As outlined in Ch.1, a person is said to be "intestate" when he dies without leaving a will or other testamentary writing to direct how his estate is to be distributed after death. However, this is not the only occasion where the rules of intestate succession are applied. The deceased could have left a will which is wholly or partly ineffective (on which see Ch.4), or someone might reject a benefit granted under a will. In some cases, a will may only dispose of part of an estate and the remainder has to be administered as though the deceased had died intestate; this is referred to as a "partial intestacy". 3–01

The lay person often assumes that the division of an estate under the rules of intestate succession is bound to be more complicated than where there is a will giving clear instructions. In fact, it is not administratively any more difficult to divide an intestate estate. In some ways it is easier, as executors must simply apply the rules; there is no will to interpret and virtually no discretion in distribution. The problem is much more social, in that the rules of division in intestacy may well not reflect what the deceased's real wishes would have been, or indeed what some family members might perceive as "fair".

Assuming payment of lawful debts and funeral expenses, the division of an intestate estate has to be considered in three successive stages. Not all stages have equal relevance in every estate (and indeed some stages may be absent entirely) but the division will always follow the order of: (1) prior rights; (2) legal rights; and (3) free estate (also known as "dead's part").

PRIOR RIGHTS

"Prior rights" is the name given to the entitlement of a surviving spouse or civil partner to make certain claims against the deceased's estate. The historical intention behind prior rights was to ensure that a surviving spouse's basic needs are provided for upon the death of his or her partner, and the specifics of the rights themselves are based on the assumption that if the deceased *had* left a will, at least part of its terms would have sought to achieve this same aim. However, this is only an assumption; if the deceased has actually left a will, even a will whose provisions are entirely contrary to the spirit of prior rights, then these assumptions are defeated and the rights do not apply. It is of utmost importance, then, to remember that prior rights only ever arise in intestate succession; they are distinct from certain other rights that are claimable by surviving family members, which will be considered in due course. 3–02

Dwellinghouse right

3–03 Under s.8(1) of the 1964 Act, the surviving spouse or civil partner is entitled to the ownership or tenancy of any one house (which includes a flatted residence) owned or tenanted by the deceased at the time of death. The house also includes any garden ground and pertinents, but not moveable property (although moveables are dealt with under another heading). The surviving spouse or civil partner must have been ordinarily resident in the house at the time of the deceased's death. However, it does not matter whether or not the deceased was ordinarily resident in the house.

The maximum value of this benefit is currently £473,000. This figure is increased from time to time by statutory instrument to take account of inflation and other factors (as are the upper limits of the other two benefits outlined below). The most recent increase at the time of writing became effective in February 2012, by way of the Prior Rights of Surviving Spouse and Civil Partner (Scotland) Order 2011. In the majority of cases, this upper limit is sufficient for the deceased's full interest to be claimed by the surviving spouse. However, in the event that the deceased's interest in the house is more than £473,000, the survivor is entitled to a sum of £473,000 only. In such situations, members of the family may come to an arrangement whereby the surviving spouse retains the house but "buys back" the excess from the estate. It may also be possible for the surviving spouse to offset the excess using other succession rights.

It is important to note that the figure refers to the value of the deceased's *interest* in the house, not to the overall value of the house itself. This is significant for two reasons. First, an ever-increasing number of dwellinghouses are jointly owned. In the case of a husband and wife who are joint (and equal) owners, the surviving spouse already enjoys an entitlement to half the overall value, and this share has no relevance to succession. It is only the deceased's share that requires to be claimed by way of prior rights. Therefore, in such cases the overall value of a dwellinghouse which would be covered by the maximum threshold can be as much as £946,000; the surviving spouse would already own £473,000 of this value and could claim the deceased's £473,000 by way of prior rights. However, this will only be the case if the house was owned by the couple outright, which leads logically to the second reason. It is possible that the deceased's interest in the house will be lower than half the total value if, for example, there is an outstanding standard security in place; in this instance it is the value of the deceased's "equity" (i.e. the value *not* subject to the standard security) that is used for prior rights purposes. For example, say Bob and Mary, a married couple, jointly own a house worth £500,000. The house was purchased with the assistance of a £350,000 loan secured by way of a standard security, £200,000 of which still remains unpaid at the time of the Bob's death. The value of Bob's interest in the house is £150,000, i.e. £500,000 total value minus the £200,000 outstanding loan amount, equalling £300,000 of equity, of which Bob owned 50 per cent, or £150,000. It is this figure that is claimed by Mary by way of her dwellinghouse rights, and she thereafter becomes solely responsible for repayment of the outstanding loan. (Although, as mentioned in Chs 1 and 2, the proceeds of a life assurance policy might be available to assist in settling this debt.)

Also of note is the fact that, in a substantial number of cases, a house may be held not only in joint names, but in joint names and the survivor. This arrangement is known as a special destination (or survivorship destination) and is explained in more detail in Ch.8. The effect of a special destination in a heritable title is to move the deceased's share, at the moment of death, to the survivor(s) without further legal formality. When this takes place, the dwellinghouse right actually has no relevance and, in cases where the deceased's share is worth more than £473,000, would actually leave the survivor in a more advantageous position.

If the house forms part of subjects included within a tenancy or where it forms part of subjects used by the deceased for the purposes of a trade, profession or occupation (such as a farm house), it cannot be claimed under the dwellinghouse right, although a cash sum in lieu would normally be payable. Occasionally, the deceased may have owned more than one house in which the survivor was ordinarily resident at the time of his death, e.g. a holiday home. In this case, the survivor has six months in which to elect (choose) which house to take.

Furniture right

Under s.8(3) of the 1964 Act, the surviving spouse or civil partner is entitled **3–04** to receive the deceased's share in the furniture and plenishings from the dwellinghouse in which the survivor was ordinarily resident, up to a value of £29,000. As with the dwellinghouse right, it does not matter whether the deceased was normally resident in the house. The value is what the furniture is worth, not what it would cost to replace it with new. Where the value of the deceased's share of the furniture is more than £29,000, the survivor may select items up to a value of £29,000. The furniture right applies even if the house itself does not form part of the intestate estate, as would happen when the heritable property passed under a special destination. The furniture right applies equally where the house was not owned by the deceased, e.g. where it was rented, always provided that the surviving spouse was ordinarily resident in it at the time of the deceased's death.

If two or more houses are involved, the survivor must, within six months of the death of the intestate, elect which lot of furniture to take. Furniture can only be taken from one house and the survivor is not allowed to "pick and mix" from the two. It is possible, however, for furniture to be taken from a different house to one claimed under the dwellinghouse right.

As well as including the most obvious categories such as furniture, carpets and curtains, the plenishings include (and the list is not exhaustive) "garden effects, domestic animals, plate, plated articles, linen, china, glass, books, pictures, prints, articles of household use and consumable stores". There is no mention of motor cars and professional practice is not to include a car as part of the furniture.

Excluded from furniture and plenishings are animals used for business purposes, money, securities and heirlooms. What might be included within the categories of heirlooms is, to use Professor Michael Meston's words, "magnificently vague". It is intended to cover items which, because of their associations rather than their value, ought to pass to the members of the deceased's family other than the surviving spouse. If these items are of purely sentimental value, this is unlikely to be contentious but if they are more valuable, the executor could be put in a somewhat difficult position.

Financial provision

3–05 Under s.9 of the 1964 Act, after the dwellinghouse and furniture rights have been satisfied, a surviving spouse or civil partner is entitled to a financial provision. Where the deceased left no surviving issue (children or further direct descendants) the maximum value of the claim is £89,000. If there are surviving issue, the maximum value is £50,000.

This provision is sometimes known as the "cash right", but it can be used to claim any property with a cash value. If both heritable and moveable property are left in the estate, the sum due will be paid proportionately from each type. If, as is quite frequently the case, there is not enough left in the estate to meet the financial provision in full, the entire remainder, heritable and moveable, is made over to the survivor.

If there is only partial intestacy and the survivor is entitled to a legacy from the estate, the financial provision must be set off against the amount of the legacy. The dwellinghouse and furniture rights do not require to be set off in this way.

Calculation of prior rights

3–06 It is worth noting that the three prior rights, although obviously considered under the one heading are, in fact, independent of one another and not merely part of a cash fund. So, what a survivor actually receives will depend very much on the mixture of assets in the estate. If someone leaves a house worth £120,000, furniture worth £10,000 and other moveables worth £170,000, the prior rights (in total) would be less than in an estate with a house valued at £145,000, furniture of £5,000 and other moveables of £150,000, despite the two estates being of equal value overall.

If any surplus of moveable property is left after payment of prior rights, the next stage would be calculation of legal rights. (As will be seen, heritable property is not relevant to legal rights; surplus heritage after prior rights would fall into the free estate.)

LEGAL RIGHTS

3–07 Legal rights are of very ancient origin in Scots law. Their application over the centuries has meant that it is not possible to totally disinherit one's spouse (now including civil partner) or children. Although mention is made of legal rights in the 1964 Act, they are very much still rooted in common law.

Strictly speaking, legal rights are not rights of succession so much as debts due from the deceased's estate (*Naismith v Boyes* (1899) 1 F. (HL) 79). It is crucial to note that they only rank against the "net moveable estate". This term refers to any moveable estate that is left after all debts, funeral expenses and administrative costs of winding up and dividing the estate have been met and prior rights (where appropriate) have also been satisfied.

Legal rights are fixed at the moment of death. They are not affected by subsequent increases or decreases in the value of the estate or by additional funds or property, such as income and dividends, subsequently coming in to the executry. Interest is deemed to accrue in the claimant's favour from date of death to date of payment at "prudent management" rate. Claiming legal rights against an intestate estate does not involve any formality since it is a basic entitlement, though it is worth noting that the rights will prescribe (expire) if they are not claimed within 20 years of their becoming enforceable.

Although legal rights are being considered here as a stage of intestate division, they apply equally to testate estates. Even if the deceased left a will, it is not possible to defeat legal rights by a testamentary provision; those entitled to them can claim legal rights regardless of a will's contents. (See Ch.5 for further discussion on this principle.) However, it is possible for anyone who should wish to do so to minimise the amount from which legal rights can be claimed, the most obvious strategy being to convert as much moveable property as possible into heritage.

Claims under legal rights

There are two legal rights: relict's part and legitim. These are their ancient **3–08**
and traditional titles; it seems likely that in time these will disappear in favour of a more generic term.

The relict's part was traditionally known either as *jus relictae* (right of the widow) or *jus relicti* (right of the widower). As mentioned above, the right now extends to a surviving civil partner. The extent of this right depends upon whether or not the deceased was also survived by issue. If the deceased left no issue, the claimant is entitled to one half of the net moveable estate. If the deceased did leave issue, the claimant is entitled to one third of the net moveable estate.

Legitim, or "bairn's part", is the right of surviving children or other direct descendants to claim against the deceased's estate. As with the relict's part, the extent of the right depends upon other survivors. If there is no surviving spouse or civil partner of the deceased, the legitim claim comprises one half of the net moveable estate. If there is a surviving spouse or civil partner, the legitim claim comprises one third of the net moveable estate. A crucial difference to note is that the "legitim fund" is *shared* amongst all claimants, so if the deceased left two children, each would be entitled to half of the fund. (This is explored in more detail below.)

Where legal rights are being claimed in the context of intestate succession (as they are being considered here), the unclaimed portion of the net moveable estate falls into the free estate. Where legal rights are being claimed in the context of testate succession, the unclaimed portion is divided according to the terms of the will. (As mentioned above, this latter situation is further considered in Ch.5.)

Representation

3–09 Before the 1964 Act came into force, only children who actually survived the deceased could have any claim against the legitim fund. This rule was logical in that it simply applied the basic rule that only those who survive the deceased may inherit. However, the rule was criticised as it failed to acknowledge arguably legitimate claims from survivors of the predeceasing legitim claimant, e.g. grandchildren of the deceased. The 1964 Act introduced the concept of "representation", which allows further issue of the deceased to claim their late parent's share.

For purposes of any legitim claim, "issue" includes not only those born within marriage but also illegitimate and adopted children. Section 21 of the Family Law (Scotland) Act 2006 abolished the status of illegitimacy, subject to certain exceptions, whilst s.23 of the 1964 Act placed adopted children in the same position as natural children in respect of their adoptive parents. It is worth noting that step-children do not qualify as issue of the deceased and so do not have any claim.

Division of the legitim fund

3–10 The manner in which the legitim fund is distributed among the claimants may be per capita (by head) or *per stirpes* (by branch). In considering the differing applications of these, it is useful to bear in mind the principle that, in general, those related most closely to the deceased have the strongest rights, which in practice tends to mean that the value of a claim is diluted as the degree of relationship to the deceased becomes more distant.

Following this logic, if all those claiming are related in the same degree to the deceased, they all have equal rights. Therefore, division is per capita, meaning each receives an equal portion. Thus, if all the claimants are surviving children, they share on a per capita basis. Similarly, if *all* the deceased's children have predeceased and *all* the claimants are grandchildren, these grandchildren are all in the same relationship to the deceased and will also share per capita.

If, on the other hand, all those claiming are not related in the same degree to the deceased, the different degrees are reflected in the value of the different claims. Therefore, division is *per stirpes*, meaning the portions received may not be equal. For instance, if there is one surviving child and another child who predeceased leaving two children, i.e. grandchildren of the deceased, the child will receive one half of the legitim fund and the grandchildren will receive one half between them, i.e. one quarter each.

Collation *inter liberos*

If a person wishes to make a claim on the legitim fund but, during the lifetime of the deceased, he received advances or gifts of moveable property, he must collate (add back) the amount of such gifts or advances into the legitim fund. The fund is then divided *inter liberos* (among the children) in the normal way. This is, in fact, a paper exercise since money is not literally paid back into the fund, it is merely taken into account in making the relevant calculations. **3–11**

There could be cases where a child has received a substantial advance and could actually be out of pocket if he were to claim legitim. He would be well advised not to make a claim, in which case he does not require to collate. In *Coats' Trustees v Coats*, 1914 S.C. 744, the only claimant on the legitim fund had received advances that were substantially less than those made to her siblings. The claimant failed in her attempt to require her siblings to collate their advances.

It is important to note that collation only applies to advances of moveable property. Thus if, say, a child is given actual heritable property, that does not require to be collated and he can make a full claim on the legitim fund. If, on the other hand, the child was given a sum of money to buy a house, that sum is clearly moveable and would require to be collated.

Certain payments are exempt from collation, e.g. sums of money expended in normal parental maintenance and provision of education. Loans made to a child do not require to be collated either, as these are actually debts due to the estate. Occasionally a parent may provide in his will that a particular advance does not require to be collated for the purposes of legitim claims, although this is unusual as most wills make provisions in lieu of legitim.

Renunciation of legitim

It is always open to any person entitled to claim legal rights to renounce his claim on the legitim fund. This has a different effect on the position of other claimants depending on whether the renunciation takes place before or after the death of the parent. **3–12**

If the discharge or renunciation takes place before the death of the parent, that claimant is deemed, for this purpose only, to have died before his parent and to have left no issue (irrespective of the true facts). The result of this renunciation is that the amount available to other claimants is bound to increase. In *Obers v Paton's Trustees (No.3)* (1897) 24 R. 719, P had been declared bankrupt. When his father was dying, P discharged his claim to legitim. This had the effect of increasing the amount available to P's siblings, simultaneously reducing P's own estate, which was being claimed by his creditors. This was an astute move, but the court actually reduced (nullified) the discharge as it was deemed prejudicial to P's creditors.

If (as is more usual) the discharge takes place after the death of the parent, the effect is quite different. As already stated, legal rights are fixed at the moment of death and nothing which takes place after the death can affect the amount designated for each claimant. In such a case, the portion of the legitim fund which has been renounced falls into the free estate or residue. It is not added to the share of other claimants against the fund.

Legal rights examples

3–13 The following examples are designed to illustrate the concepts outlined above. In all cases it is presumed that debts and prior rights have already been settled.

Simple legal rights example

3–14 Henry dies intestate, survived by his wife Wilma, son Stephen and daughter Deborah. Henry's net moveable estate is £60,000.

Wilma's *jus relictae* right entitles her to 1/3 of the net moveable estate, i.e. £20,000.

Stephen and Deborah collectively are entitled to share in the legitim fund. This comprises 1/3 of the net moveable estate, or £20,000. Since Stephen and Deborah are both related to Henry by the same degree (i.e. they are both his children), they will divide the legitim fund per capita, giving each £10,000.

Since Henry is intestate, the final 1/3 is free estate and will be distributed accordingly.

Example of division per stirpes

3–15 Henry dies intestate, survived by his wife Wilma, son Stephen and grandchildren George and Greta from his pre-deceased daughter, Deborah. Henry's net moveable estate is £60,000.

Wilma's *jus relictae* right entitles her to 1/3 of the net moveable estate, i.e. £20,000.

Stephen, George and Greta collectively are entitled to share in the legitim fund, which is also £20,000. However, since the claimants are not all related to the deceased by the same degree, the fund must be divided *per stirpes*. Stephen is entitled to half the fund, whilst George and Greta are entitled to share the other half. Therefore, Stephen receives £10,000, whilst George and Greta receive £5,000 each.

Example of division per capita

3–16 Henry dies intestate, survived by his six grandchildren, four born to his pre-deceased son, Stephen, and two born to his pre-deceased daughter, Deborah. His wife Wilma also pre-deceased him, although she is survived by a son, Simon, from a previous relationship. Henry's net moveable estate is £60,000.

Wilma has pre-deceased so there is no *jus relictae* claim. Wilma's son Simon (i.e. Henry's step-son) has no claim; representation does not apply to *jus relictae*, and step-children do not qualify as legitim claimants.

All six grandchildren are entitled to share in the legitim fund, which comprises 1/2 of the net moveable estate (since there is no *jus relictae* claim), i.e. £30,000. Since all legitim claimants are in the same degree of relationship to the deceased (i.e. all are his grandchildren), division is per capita, giving each £5,000. It does not matter that four grandchildren have come from one "branch" and two have come from another.

Example of collation

Henry dies intestate, survived by his son Stephen and daughter Deborah. **3–17** His wife, Wilma, pre-deceased him. Henry's net moveable estate is £60,000. However, three years before his death Henry gave Stephen £6,000 in order to pay off a business debt.

Wilma has pre-deceased so there is no *jus relictae* claim.

Stephen and Deborah collectively are entitled to share in the legitim fund, which is 1/2 of the net moveable estate, i.e. £30,000. However, if Stephen wishes to claim, he must collate the £6,000. This means that the legitim fund is actually £36,000 for the purposes of calculation. The fund will then be divided in the normal way among the claimants (per capita since both are children), meaning each is entitled to £18,000. Stephen has already had £6,000, so he will receive a further £12,000 from the estate, bringing his total benefit to £18,000. Deborah will receive her £18,000 directly from the estate, meaning that each child has, overall, received an equal benefit.

Example of renunciation

Henry dies intestate, survived by his wife Wilma, son Stephen and daughter **3–18** Deborah. Henry's net moveable estate is £60,000.

Wilma's *jus relictae* right entitles her to 1/3 of the net moveable estate, i.e. £20,000.

Stephen and Deborah collectively are entitled to share in the legitim fund, which is also 1/3 of the net moveable estate, i.e. £20,000. Each would be entitled to £10,000.

If Stephen had renounced his legal rights before Henry died, he would be treated as having pre-deceased without issue. He would therefore be excluded from the legitim fund, which would be claimed in its entirety by Deborah, i.e. she would receive £20,000.

If, however, Stephen renounced his legal rights after Henry's death, the outcome would be different. Because legal rights are fixed at the moment of death, Deborah's share of the legitim fund cannot be increased by Stephen's post-death actions. She will therefore receive one half of the fund (£10,000), just as if Stephen had accepted his share. The £10,000 which Stephen has rejected will fall into the free estate.

FREE ESTATE

3–19 The balance that remains after the satisfaction of both prior and legal rights is the free estate or "dead's part". It may contain heritable and moveable property. From what has already been demonstrated, it stands to reason that if someone dies intestate, with no surviving spouse, civil partner or children, his entire estate is free estate.

It is crucial to understand that free estate can only be claimed in the event of intestacy. A claim to free estate is *not* like a claim for legal rights which can, as mentioned above, prevail against a will. Thus, siblings and other members of the family have no claim to the free estate if the deceased made a valid will. It might be upsetting if, say, a bachelor leaves all his property to the local Cats' Home but, in such circumstances, his extended family members have no legal claim of succession to any part of the estate.

The 1964 Act lays down the order of succession to the free estate. In essence, it is simple: the executor will look at each successive "class" of relations in the under-noted list. As soon as he strikes a class in which there is a possible claimant, he stops there and goes no further. This is the class to whom, or among whom, the free estate falls to be divided. Representation applies, unless indicated to the contrary. There is no provision for cohabitees, whose position is outlined below. The rules on division per capita or *per stirpes* are exactly the same as for legal rights.

The order of distribution is as follows:

(1) children;
(2) parents (no representation) *and* siblings together, provided there is at least one of each—each class shares one half of the free estate;
(3) siblings, where there is no surviving parent;
(4) parents (no representation), where there are no surviving siblings;
(5) spouse or civil partner (no representation);
(6) uncles and aunts, whether maternal or paternal;
(7) grandparents;
(8) great uncles and great aunts;
(9) remoter ancestors;
(10) the Crown.

The effect of this list is that there is representation in respect of the descending and collateral lines, but none in respect of parents and spouses. Collaterals (such as brothers and sisters or uncles and aunts) of the full-blood (sharing both parents with the intestate or an ancestor) exclude those of the half-blood (sharing one parent with the intestate or an ancestor). However, in the case of half-blood, it makes no difference whether the shared parent was mother or father. A step-brother or step-sister has no claim on the estate.

Subject to the two exceptions to representation, it does not matter how remote the relationship is, nor does it matter whether it was legitimate or illegitimate, to use the older concepts. If, after working through the above list, no relation can be found, the estate will go to the Crown as *ultimus haeres* (final heir). An official with the impressive title of the Queen's and Lord Treasurer's Remembrancer takes possession of the estate, pays debts and must advertise for possible relatives. If none are forthcoming any balance will be applied to the Treasury. In carrying out his duties, the Remembrancer has an element of discretion, not open to an executor of an intestate estate. For example, he could make a financial payment to, say, a companion or retainer of the deceased.

EXAMPLE OF INTESTATE DIVISION

A husband dies leaving a widow, one son and one daughter. His net estate is £220,000, made up of dwellinghouse (£160,000), furniture (£4,000) and investments of £56,000. (Note that figures in brackets indicate deductions from the estate, and "NME" refers to "net moveable estate".) **3–20**

	Heritable	**Moveable**
Estate		
Dwellinghouse	160,000	
Furniture		4,000
Investments		56,000
Balances	160,000	60,000
Deduct prior rights		
Dwellinghouse	(160,000)	
Furniture		(4,000)
Financial provision		(50,000)
Balances	Nil	6,000
Deduct legal rights		
Relict's part 1/3 NME		(2,000)
Legitim 1/3 NME		(2,000)
Balances	Nil	2,000
Deduct free estate		
To children		(2,000)
Balances	Nil	Nil

The final distribution would be:

Widow	
Prior Rights	£214,000
Relict's part	£2,000
TOTAL	£216,000

Son	
1/2 Legitim	£1,000
1/2 Free estate	£1,000
TOTAL	£2,000

Daughter	
1/2 Legitim	£1,000
1/2 Free estate	£1,000
TOTAL	£2,000

The above example is one of classic simplicity. Notice that even in this case, where there are sufficient funds to make a legitim payment, the lion's share of the estate passes to the widow.

COHABITING COUPLES

3–21 There is nothing new about couples cohabiting. Although perhaps frowned upon in some circles, couples have been living together without formalising their relationship for hundreds of years. The term "common law marriage" is often employed, but this imprecise expression has never been recognised under Scots law and is best avoided. The similar concept of "irregular marriage" has, however, long been recognised in Scotland. This allowed parties who had cohabited with each other as husband and wife, with the general reputation of being so, to make an application to the court for a declarator confirming constitution of their marriage. This would allow a successful claimant to acquire full succession rights (and certain other property rights). Under similar provisions the court may recognise as valid a marriage entered into abroad where, unknown to the parties, the marriage was invalid under the law of that country.

Irregular marriage was virtually abolished by the Family Law (Scotland) Act 2006 ("the 2006 Act"). In its place, the 2006 Act introduced groundbreaking rights for cohabiting couples. A surviving cohabitant can make a claim on their partner's estate, but only if the deceased is intestate. If the deceased left a valid will, then the surviving cohabitant cannot make a claim (although any benefits granted under the will can, of course, be taken).

For the purposes of succession and property rights, s.25 of the 2006 Act defines a cohabitant as a person who is or was living with another person as if they were husband and wife, or as if they were civil partners. In determining this, the court shall have regard to a number of factors, such as: the length of time during which the two persons lived together; the nature of their relationship; and the nature and extent of any financial arrangements between them.

Under s.29 of the 2006 Act, the court has discretion to make any award, such as a capital payment or transfer of property, up to the amount that the claimant would have been entitled to if the parties had been married or in a civil partnership. In determining this amount, the court shall consider factors such as the size of the estate, any other benefits received by the claimant, and any other claims made on the estate.

Although relatively new legislation, the provisions of the 2006 Act in this regard have been subject to a fair amount of judicial interpretation. Length of cohabitation was considered in *Chebotareva v Khandro*, 2008 Fam. L.R. 66, where it was remarked that a period exceeding one year would be sufficient. Factors affecting the amount were relevant in *Savage v Purches*, 2009 S.L.T. (Sh. Ct) 36, where the claimant's action failed on the basis that he had already received a substantial lump sum from the death benefit of the deceased's pension. The balance of interests as between a cohabitant and children of the deceased was considered by the court in *Windram, Applicant*, 2009 Fam. L.R. 157, in which a substantial capital payment was awarded to the applicant, who had cohabited with the deceased for a period of 24 years.

Finally here, it is crucial to appreciate that a cohabitant's rights are not the equivalent of a spouse or civil partner's legal rights. They are perhaps more in keeping with prior rights, although even here there is a distinction since a cohabitant's rights are not automatic. The Scottish Law Commission has recommended that the rights of cohabitees in succession should be further reformed by a new statutory regime, which would extend also to claims made against a testate estate. As yet no such change has been implemented.

4. MAKING A WILL

4–01 Many a good story, whether taken from the classics or popular yarns, centres around a will. Did the deceased make a will? If so, where is it? If he made such a will, was he of sound mind when he made it? Why, if he was of sound mind, did he decide to leave all his money to the Cats' Home? Is the deceased trying to get even with his family from beyond the grave?

The reader may even have seen old movies which feature a formal reading of the will, usually on a wet afternoon after the funeral and often bringing an unpleasant surprise to the members of the deceased's family by naming an entirely unexpected main beneficiary! Such scenes make great theatre, but in fact formal readings of a will virtually never take place in practice.

THE PURPOSE AND BENEFITS OF A WILL

4–02 As stated in the previous chapter, the average lay person might perceive that there will be fewer complications in the event of someone dying testate than intestate. This has an element of truth in it, but it is not the whole truth. If a party dies intestate, the rules of intestate succession have to be applied. It has been demonstrated that there are few grey areas in the rules of intestate succession and there is little or no room for flexibility, subject to the judicial discretion which may be applied in the case of a surviving cohabitant.

In the case of testate succession, there is the obvious advantage that people know where they stand. It makes sense to have a clear will, professionally framed and properly signed, and then to ensure that it is regularly updated. The great majority of wills present no problems and prevent many from arising. Yet there is more potential for matters to go wrong, even if this only happens in a small minority of cases. Most estates falling under testate succession are wound up uneventfully. Nevertheless, anyone working in the legal environment always has to be prepared for the unexpected.

The law of testate succession deals with the disposal, on death, of property by means of a will or other testamentary writing. If a will creates a trust, this trust continues beyond the actual executry of the estate and the document is usually known as a "trust disposition and settlement".

One obvious problem with testate succession is that no two wills are ever identical, even if many are very similar. It is important, when making a will, that testators consider as many eventualities as possible, even those which may be less pleasant. Parents do not normally expect to outlive their children, and whilst it may be painful to consider a child or other younger beneficiary predeceasing, it is always a possibility. Traditionally, the average married man assumes that he will die before his wife, and statistics consistently suggest that there is some merit in that assumption. However, people do not always die in what might be seen as the "natural" order.

There are few actual rules about what people cannot do by will. It was mentioned in Ch.3 that no one can exclude valid claims to legal rights by a spouse, civil partner or children. This, along with other matters relating to will conditions, is further considered in Ch.5. The main focus of what follows is on the preparation and execution of a will, rather than its contents.

VALIDITY OF WILLS

A will, or testamentary settlement, is a *written* declaration of what a person wishes to be done with his estate after death. There are no special forms of words and the reader will have to look long and hard to find any professionally drafted will which begins with the words, "I, being of sound mind and body . . ."; save that for the movies referred to above. **4–03**

One of the most common failings in home-made wills is that often they import half-understood jargon from books, novels and films. In practice, it is much safer to refer to "children" than "issue", because, as mentioned in Ch.1, issue means not only children but also all direct descendants. Yet, to some people, "issue" sounds more impressive. The other main failing concerns the formal validity of the document.

It is perfectly true that a will can competently be written on the back of a cigarette packet, although this is hardly the most respectful way of treating potential beneficiaries. Any document that gives rise to obligations requires to be signed; in other words it must be "formally valid". This is different from a document being "essentially valid", which concerns the essence of the document (i.e. what it purports to do), or which may refer to some external factor which is not immediately obvious, such as lack of capacity on the part of the granter.

Essential validity

The testator must have the necessary capacity in law to "test", i.e. to make a valid will. To put it another way, the law must recognise that he is able to dispose of property *mortis causa* (on account of death) at the time the will is made. Any person, male or female, aged 12 years or over can test (Age of Legal Capacity (Scotland) Act 1991 s.2(2)). Someone of unsound mind does not have capacity to test. If the testator, though affected by mental illness, had lucid intervals, he might still have the power to form the necessary intention (*Nisbet's Trustees v Nisbet* (1871) 9 M. 937). **4–04**

The law presumes in favour of mental capacity, unless the testator has been subject to an order under mental health legislation. Evidence must be led to rebut this presumption. Delusion and abnormal eccentricity do not constitute lack of capacity; generations of students have been introduced to the case of *Morrison v Maclean's Trustees* (1862) 24 D. 625, where an eccentric testator's will was held to be valid, despite the fact that much of his everyday speech had been of an obscene and bizarre nature and that he claimed to have been fed from an eagle's nest when young. Similarly, in the more recent case of *Stewart v Franks* [2013] CSOH 63, paranoid and abusive behaviour by the testator towards his family members was not accepted as sufficient evidence of incapacity.

Capacity to test might also be affected by facility and circumvention or undue influence. "Facility" is not an easy state to define. It certainly falls short of mental unsoundness but means that a person is easily manipulated by others (*Gibson's Executor v Anderson*, 1925 S.C. 774). A facility might occur in someone who is elderly or, for whatever reason, feeble-minded. In itself, facility might not be enough to make a will invalid, particularly if the provisions of the will are clear in themselves. For the will to be open to challenge, there also needs to be an element of circumvention, i.e. "getting round" the testator to influence him to make provisions harmful to his interests.

Undue influence is different from facility and circumvention, but the distinction is sometimes easier to state than to apply in practice. There is no need to show that the testator suffered any form of facility. Rather, there will be some relationship of trust and confidence between the beneficiary and the testator, even if this relationship is not generally one giving rise to legal duties. Examples would be parent to child (and vice versa), solicitor to client, doctor to patient, or even an art dealer to a customer (*Honeyman's Executor v Sharp*, 1978 S.C. 223). People can, of course, be influenced for good as much as for ill and the law does not seek to interfere in the giving of reasonable advice or counsel to potential testators. The possibility of challenge would only arise if it could be shown that a testator's intention had been in some way overborne.

Formal validity

4–05 The first elementary, but crucial, matter to note is that a will requires to be in writing. Even if someone, on his death bed, states that he is changing his will, this is of no significance unless the new provision is put into writing and properly signed as explained below. It is not possible (at least yet) to execute a valid will by means of recording other than writing, such as video or electronic communication.

Having established that a written document exists, a crucial distinction is whether it was signed before 1st August 1995, or on or after this date. This is the date on which the Requirements of Writing (Scotland) Act 1995 ("the 1995 Act") came into force, significantly changing the law in this area. The two legal positions are now considered in turn.

Wills executed before 1st August 1995

4–06 There are likely to still be a fair number of wills executed before the above date by people who are still alive. This means that the old law will continue to be relevant for a considerable period of time. Under the old law, a nuncupative (verbal) legacy of not more than £100 Scots (£8.33) was valid, but this provision is obsolete and has no modern relevance.

Pre-1995 practice was governed partly by common law and partly by ancient statute. The statutory provisions were found in a venerable collection of Acts of the Scots Parliament, interpreted over the years by the courts and partly modernised by 19th and 20th century legislation, known by the august collective title of the "Authentication Statutes".

For wills executed under the old law, before an executor can obtain confirmation on the basis of the will, it requires to be in "probative form". This basically means that the court will presume that the execution (signature) of the document is valid, unless it can be proved to the contrary. In practice, it requires fairly convincing proof to overturn a probative document.

At Scottish common law, a will was regarded as valid if it was handwritten and signed by the testator. This is known as a "holograph" will. Such a will is not regarded as probative; rather it is said to be "privileged". This means that it can be given the status of probativity if the writing and signature can be proved to be that of the testator. Proof is by way of two affidavits. In practice, the courts have accepted some very informal testamentary writings and, in context, even signatures in "pet" names, e.g. "Connie" (*Draper v Thomason*, 1954 S.C. 136) or "Mum" (*Rhodes v Peterson*, 1972 S.L.T. 98). It is also possible for a typed document, or one prepared by someone else, to be "adopted as holograph" by the testator, although this must be expressly stated in the testator's own handwriting. A typed document with a signature would not normally be deemed sufficient (*Chisholm v Chisholm*, 1949 S.C. 434), although in the unusual case of *McBeath's Trustees v McBeath*, 1935 S.C. 471, the court held a fully typed will to be valid, on the grounds that the testator's disability meant that typing was his normal form of writing.

The more usual form of probativity under the old law is where the will is attested, which means subscribed (signed) on every page by the testator and witnessed by two individuals (who also sign). If there is a minor informality of execution, such as omitting to sign one of the pages, it is possible to ask the court for this informality to be cured under s.39 of the Conveyancing (Scotland) Act 1874. However, a more serious defect could be fatal to the will. In the case of *Williamson v Williamson*, 1997 S.L.T. 1044, Mrs Williamson had signed her will in 1988. The two witnesses were Mr Wilson and his wife. In a fit of absent-mindedness and in the heat of the moment, Mr Wilson accidentally signed his surname as "Williamson". After Mrs Williamson's death, a member of her family noticed this obvious inconsistency and challenged the validity of the will; it was declared invalid and the estate fell into intestacy.

Wills executed on or after 1st August 1995

As stated above, the 1995 Act changed the law significantly in this area, but **4–07**
only affects documents or deeds executed after it came into force. If a document is undated, it is treated as having been executed under the new

law. The changes as they affect the execution of a will are not particularly radical. Small nuncupative legacies disappeared, although in practice they had long since gone without trace. The privileged status of a holograph will also disappeared; as explained below, there is no longer any reason for retaining its status.

The basis of the post-1995 law is that any document is formally valid if it is subscribed by the granter. (The 1995 Act applies to various legal documents; wills constitute just one aspect of its application.) Thus, it does not matter whether a will is handwritten, typed, printed, word processed or a mixture of the above: provided the will is signed at the end, it is formally valid. This fail-safe provision was greatly welcomed. Signatures can include marks and "pet" names, but these may require to be fortified by evidence that it was the granter's usual manner of signing or that it was intended, in context, as a signature.

There is still, however, the further hurdle of probativity to be crossed. In the post-1995 language, a will requires to be "self proving" if it is to be used as the basis for administration of the estate. (This is more or less the equivalent of probative under the old law.) In other words, if there is any challenge to the execution of the document, the court will presume it to be genuine until the opposite is proved. For a will to have this status, it should be signed on every page by the testator, and the signature should be attested by one witness.

If a will is produced after the testator's death which is formally valid but not self proving, by this time it is obviously too late to have it signed on every sheet and witnessed. However, all is not lost. An application can be made to the court for the will to be given self proving status. Evidence that the signature was that of the deceased must be provided by affidavit of two appropriate persons. This is essentially the same process under which a holograph will would previously have been made probative.

Though subtle, the differences between the two regimes, and the improvements brought about by the 1995 Act, can be demonstrated with reference to the *Williamson* case discussed above. If the *Williamson* will had been executed under the new law, it would have fared much better. Even though the attestation had been botched, the will would still have stood as formally valid. It could then have been given self proving status, which would have prevented the estate falling into intestacy.

Vicarious subscription

4–08 There may be times when someone wishes to sign a will but for some reason is unable to write. This might be due to blindness or physical incapacity and may be temporary or permanent. In such cases, someone else may subscribe vicariously, i.e. sign on the testator's behalf. This situation is potentially very delicate and so stringent rules must be applied to avoid, or at least greatly reduce, the possibility of fraud.

Under the old law, the procedure was known as notarial execution. This allowed the document to be signed on the testator's behalf by a solicitor, notary public or parish minister of the Church of Scotland. If the vicarious subscriber had any interest in the will, however fair and above board, this was fatal and the subscription, and thus the entire will, was invalid (*Ferrie v Ferrie's Trustees* (1863) 1 M. 291). Also, the actual procedure, which involved a docket being handwritten onto the document before two witnesses, had to be meticulously observed to the letter, otherwise the entire will could be invalid.

The 1995 Act made the procedure somewhat more user-friendly. A "relevant person" may undertake the vicarious subscription, i.e. a practising solicitor, advocate, justice of the peace or sheriff clerk. A witness must be present throughout. The will should be read over to the testator, though this requirement can be waived if he so wishes; this fact should be declared in the testing clause. There is no separate handwritten docket as there was with notarial execution. If the document is to be self proving, it should be vicariously subscribed on every page. The witness must see the granter give authority to subscribe and either hear the document being read in full or hear the granter dispense with the reading. The "relevant person" should have no interest in the deed. If it confers a money benefit directly or indirectly on the relevant person or his immediate family, that particular benefit is invalid; however, the remainder of the document will stand.

Will forms

It is possible to buy will forms from stationers with certain words already **4–09**
pre-printed. The testator fills in the blanks, in relation to appointment of an executor, legacies and suchlike. One of the most common problems is that many of these forms are designed for English law, although there are Scottish versions available. Lawyers, of course, do not like them. Certainly, in the wrong hands they can be dangerous weapons.

If, under the old law, such a form was properly signed and witnessed, then the fact that it is partly written and partly printed does not create any problem in itself. The real problem arises where a will form, signed under the old law, was neither adopted nor attested. It would be possible to regard the parts written in the testator's own handwriting as a holograph will in themselves provided, when read separately, the words could make testamentary sense. In the case of *McDonald v Cuthbertson* (1890) 18 R. 101, a testator made an unwitnessed will on a printed will form. Reading the printed and handwritten parts together, the will made perfect sense but there was no way in which the handwritten parts on their own made any sense, testamentary or otherwise. The will was invalid. In the later case of *Carmichael's Executors v Carmichael*, 1909 S.C. 1387, all the vital words were holograph and it was possible to deduce intelligible intentions from them.

As explained above, under the post-1995 position it makes no difference if a document is handwritten, printed or (as will likely be the case with a form will) a mixture of the two.

INTENTION TO TEST

4–10 Occasionally, a problem may arise in knowing whether a document is actually a will or merely an instruction to another party to draw up a will, or even just a statement of future intention. Crucially, the document would have to pass the tests of formal validity, outlined above, before the court could declare it to be a will. The court would also have to be satisfied that there was testamentary intention, but does not look for any particular form of language. Thus in the *Rhodes* case (*Rhodes v Peterson*, 1972 S.L.T. 98), a mother's letter to her daughter outlining testamentary provisions was held to be a will.

If the document is headed "draft" or "rough", as in *Sprot's Trustees v Sprot*, 1909 S.C. 272, it will not be counted as a will. The courts have traditionally been less exacting in their standards when considering holograph or home-made wills. A document which appears to express testamentary intention or which gives instructions to a person other than a law agent is much more likely to be accepted as a will than an instruction to a law agent. In *Ayrshire Hospice, Petitioners,* 1993 S.L.T. (Sh. Ct) 75, a lady had written a three page document in her own handwriting. It contained a list of legacies to relatives, prefixed by the word "To". The final page referred to "remainder" and gave a list of charities. The document was found in an envelope on which were printed the words "Will of…". In context, this was a valid will. Conversely, in the old case of *Munro v Coutts* (1813) 1 Dow 437, a testator sent a letter to his law agent enclosing an apparently valid holograph provision with an instruction to engross it as a codicil. This was held to be no more than an instruction and not a testamentary document.

EXAMPLES OF WILLS

4–11 The following examples are intended to illustrate some of the concepts outlined above. Commentary is provided following each example.

Example 1

4–12 The first document is in the form of a handwritten letter as follows:

26 Elm Way
Grimburgh
10 August 1994

Dear Jim,

As you are my only brother and I have no husband or children of my own, I am relying on you to see that my affairs are properly sorted out after I've gone.

I would like you to have my house and the furniture as well, apart from the painting of the Town Hall, which I would like you to give to the local museum.

As for the rest of my stuff—my savings in the bank, my shares and so on—

you can divide it up among your girls.

By the way, Jim, I don't want that wife of yours to get her hands on anything of mine.

Anyway, Jim, thanks so much for being a good brother.

Your ever loving and devoted sister

Beenie

Whilst it is not a masterpiece of draughtsmanship, the above is almost certainly a valid will. It is written, signed and clearly has a testamentary intention. It is a holograph will, which requires affidavit evidence that it is in the handwriting of the deceased. Jim appears to be appointed as executor nominate, although more by implication than by express appointment. In a will, for reasons which are explained in Ch.7, it is better to avoid words such as "like" and go for stronger verbs such as "instruct" or "direct". Her "stuff" is not adequately described, neither is it clear who Jim's "girls" are. If one daughter were to predecease, did she wish her share to be added on to that of the others or would it fall into intestacy? The gratuitous comment about Jim's wife would have been better left unsaid. As she is not a beneficiary, she will not inherit directly.

If the letter had been signed under the present law, it would be formally valid as it is subscribed by the granter, but there would require to be evidence led that "Beenie" was actually her signature. If the will had been undated, it would be presumed to be executed under the present law.

Example 2

The second will is typewritten and signed: **4–13**

I, ALBERT ALEXANDER HIGGINS, residing at Eleven Railway Cuttings, Coalburgh, in order to settle my affairs after my death, do hereby leave and bequeath all my means and estate, heritable and moveable, real and personal, wheresoever situated to my wife LETITIA HIGGINS, residing with me at Eleven Railway Cuttings aforesaid; and I appoint my said wife to be my executrix.

Albert A. Higgins
28 August 1994

Unfortunately, this is not a valid will, although it is perfectly clear and uses professional language. It was signed under the old law and, to be valid, it should have been attested or holograph or adopted as holograph. As it is none of these, it is not valid.

If it were signed under the present law, or if it were undated, it would fair much better. Since it is signed it would be formally valid, although affidavit evidence would be required to fortify the signature in any application for it to be given self proving status.

Example 3

4–14 The third will is also typewritten and signed:

I, *JON SMYTH, residing at Six Union Square, Aberdeen in order to provide for the succession to my means and estate in the event of my death do hereby leave and bequeath my whole estate both heritable and moveable to my wife DOROTHY, residing with me at Six Union Square aforesaid provided that she survive me by thirty clear days; declaring that in the event of my wife predeceasing me or failing to survive me by thirty clear days I leave and bequeath my said estate equally between my children ALFRED and JOHN; and I declare that it is my wish to be buried with my parents and grandparents in Nellfield Cemetery; And I revoke my former testamentary writings: IN WITNESS WHEREOF I have subscribed these presents at Aberdeen on the Fifth day of August Nineteen Hundred and Ninety Four before these witnesses, Charles Cooper and Jean Donald, both clerks in the employment of Messrs Robb and Steele, Advocates in Aberdeen.*

J. Smyth

C. Cooper Witness

John Donald Witness

This will looks okay at first glance but, on closer inspection, it can be seen that there is something wrong with the attestation. The testing clause names "Jean Donald" as a witness whereas the signature is clearly "John Donald". Assuming that all the parties have signed their correct names, the will is not probative because, under the old law, two correctly identified witnesses required to sign. However, an error of this type in a testing clause could be counted as an informality of execution, curable by s.39 procedure. This is different from the *Williamson* case where one of the witnesses actually failed to sign his correct name.

If it were signed under present law, it would be formally valid and self proving, since only one witness is required. The informality in terms of the second witness would not be relevant.

5. TESTAMENTARY PROVISIONS

The law generally presumes in favour of a testator's freedom. Even in today's complex and highly regulated society, people may generally do as they please with their own property when alive. Similarly, they can decide how to dispose of it after death. As mentioned in Ch.3, the important exception to this proposition is found in legal rights, since they can never be defeated by a will (this issue is considered later in this chapter). **5–01**

Once a potential testator has decided in principle what he wishes to be done with his estate after death, the obvious next step should be to consult with a solicitor so that an appropriate will can be drawn up and signed. It is not surprising that some parts of a professionally drafted will are in formal legal jargon but most simple modern wills are perfectly easy for a lay person to understand. The language of a will is intended to avoid confusion, not to create it.

There are a number of very commonly-encountered testamentary provisions which will comprise the majority of most wills, particularly those that have been drafted under professional legal supervision. There are also some more unusual provisions found in the world of testate succession, a number of which the law will not tolerate.

COMMON PROVISIONS IN A WILL

Most testators are not too concerned about what they cannot do by will; they merely want to provide a fair and just settlement of their affairs after death. In practice, many testators make quite simple wills, perhaps leaving all property to a spouse or civil partner, or to children, or to other close relatives. It may even be the case that a favourite charity benefits from the entirety of an estate. In other cases, the testator may wish to make more detailed provisions, often by way of: (1) legacy; (2) annuity; or (3) liferent and fee. These will now be examined in turn. **5–02**

LEGACIES

A legacy is a bequest of property and is by far the most commonly encountered will provision. The "subject" of the legacy is the property to be bequeathed, and the "object" is the recipient, also known as the "legatee". **5–03**

Legacies can be divided into three main categories: special, general or residuary. A special (or specific) legacy is, as the name would suggest, a bequest of a specific item such as a house, a grandfather clock or "my shares in Black & White Plc".

A general legacy is one in which the subject matter of the item has no distinct individual character of its own to distinguish it from others of the same kind. The easiest and most common example is a sum of money, e.g. "the sum of £5,000". It could also be a quantity of goods coming under a generic or general description.

The residue of the estate is whatever is left after the special and general legacies are paid in full. Obviously, the amount of residue will vary greatly, depending on what is included in the estate. A residuary legatee could receive nothing or next to nothing, or could receive a very large amount. In many cases, it falls somewhere in between.

These categories are not merely artificial. The executor must pay the legacies in the order of special first, followed by general and lastly the residue.

Legacies example

5–04 Peggy Sue, a widow with no children, has died. In her will, which has been validly executed, she makes the following provisions:

1. Her house and all furniture therein is to go to her brother Bill;
2. Her wedding ring is to go to her niece, Maggie;
3. Her car is to go to her nephew, Jimmy;
4. £10,000 in cash is to go to Bill;
5. £5,000 in cash is to go to Maggie;
6. £5,000 in cash is to go to Jimmy;
7. £1,000 in cash is to go to the local Cat & Dog Home;
8. Any remainder is to be donated to the local church fund.

Peggy Sue's net estate is £216,000, comprising her house (£175,000), furniture (£8,500) wedding ring (£1,000), car (£1,500), and other moveable property amounting to £30,000. It can be seen that in her will she makes three special legacies, four general legacies, and one residual legacy. These would be dealt with in order as outlined in the table below. (Figures in brackets indicate deductions from the estate.)

	Heritable	**Moveable**
Estate		
House	175,000	
Furniture		8,500
Wedding ring		1,000
Car		1,500
Other moveable estate		30,000
Balances	175,000	41,000
Deduct special legacies		
House	(175,000)	
Furniture		(8,500)

Wedding ring		(1,000)
Car		(1,500)
Balances	Nil	30,000
Deduct general legacies		
£10,000 to Bill		(10,000)
£5,000 to Maggie		(5,000)
£5,000 to Jimmy		(5,000)
£1,000 to Cat & Dog home		(1,000)
Balances	Nil	9,000
Deduct residue		
Residue to Church fund		(9,000)
Balances	Nil	Nil

The final distribution would be:

Bill	
Special legacies	£183,500
General legacy	£10,000
TOTAL	£193,500
Maggie	
Special legacy	£1,000
General legacy	£5,000
TOTAL	£6,000
Jimmy	
Special legacy	£1,500
General legacy	£5,000
TOTAL	£6,500
Cat & Dog Home	
General legacy	£1,000
Church fund	
Residue	£9,000

In this example, the residuary legatee has been left with a substantial amount; a sum greater, in fact, than most of the other legatees. However, this should not suggest that the residual legatee will always be in such a favourable position. In fact, in theory at least, the opposite is true, since the residuary legatee will only inherit if there is property left over to allow this. Since the residuary legatee is paid last, it is very possible that special and general legacies will exhaust the estate, therefore leaving the residuary legatee with nothing at all.

Indeed, there are also a number of situations in which the estate falls short in some other way, e.g. because there are insufficient funds to satisfy every legacy, or if a special legacy attempts to bequeath an item no longer belonging to the testator. These issues are remedied by two mechanisms known as "abatement" and "ademption".

Abatement

5–05 A problem can arise when, even although the estate is solvent (i.e. all debts can be paid), there is not enough left to pay every beneficiary named in the will. This problem is dealt with by bringing in certain presumptions (unless the will expressly provides otherwise) and these presumptions are known as the rules on "abatement", or "cutting back".

Special legacies must be paid first and in full, even if there is not sufficient to pay general legatees in full. Thus a special legatee, in many ways, is in the best position.

General legacies are paid next. If there are not sufficient monies to pay them in full, general legacies are "abated pari passu" (cut back in equal proportion). To achieve this, the shortfall of the estate must be calculated as a percentage, and this percentage is then applied to each general legacy. For example, if the estate is short by 20 per cent, each general legacy is cut back by 20 per cent, thus ensuring that every general legatee is treated fairly.

Lastly, the residue is due to be paid over. Of course, if there is nothing left, the residuary legatee gets nothing. To put this another way, the residue is the first class of legacies to be abated, even although in practice it is last to be paid.

Continuing the practical example from above might help to illustrate the principle of abatement, which admittedly appears complicated at first but is actually relatively straightforward.

Staying with Peggy Sue, then, say the facts of the situation are exactly as before, but instead of Peggy Sue's estate including £30,000 of moveable estate, it includes only £15,750. Special legacies are unaffected by this change, so they are paid out exactly as before; Bill takes the house and furniture, Maggie takes the wedding ring and Jimmy takes the car. However, there is a problem with the general legacies, which (according to Peggy Sue's will) should total £21,000. As there is only £15,750 of moveable estate available to pay these general legacies, there is a shortfall of £5,250, or 25 per cent. Therefore, each general legacy will be abated by

25 per cent; Bill will receive £7,500 of his general legacy, Maggie and Jimmy will each receive £3,750, and the Cat & Dog Home will receive £750. The church fund, as residuary legatee, gets nothing at all, since its legacy is abated first and in full. (Residual legacies are considered in more detail later in this chapter.)

Ademption of special legacies

Where a testator provides for a special legacy and, at the date of his death, **5–06** the subject of the legacy no longer forms part of his estate, the legacy is said to be "adeemed" (the noun is ademption) and nothing is due to the legatee. The motives of the testator in disposing of the item are irrelevant. Thus if Peggy Sue leaves her car to her nephew Jimmy but at the date of her death no longer owns that car, Jimmy's legacy lapses and nothing is due to him under this heading.

Occasionally, a testator may leave something in his will which never belonged to him (as distinct from an article which did once belong to him but of which he has disposed). This is different from ademption and is known as *legatum rei alienae* (legacy of a thing belonging to someone else). The normal presumption is that the testator made a mistake and, accordingly, the legacy fails. However, if it can be proved that the testator knew that the property was not his, then the legacy can be interpreted as an instruction to buy the item from its owner or, if it cannot be bought, to hand over the value to the legatee. Fairly obviously, it may be difficult, if not impossible, to prove what the testator knew.

ANNUITIES

An annuity is the right to a periodical fixed payment of a sum of money **5–07** from the revenue of the estate. It can also be used to signify an arrangement with a financial institution in which, in return for a capital sum, an income is paid, usually for the remainder of a person's life. At this stage, we are confining ourselves to the first alternative. An annuity may be created in favour of any person either inter vivos (taking effect during the lifetime of the granter) or mortis causa (taking effect upon the granter's death, i.e. under a will). The annuity may be for any sum that the granter wishes and may continue as long as he desires. The most common practice is to provide an annuity for a beneficiary for his or her lifetime but it should be noted that the granter may fix the period for a shorter time. There may even be a provision that the annuity will terminate should some particular event take place, such as the re-marriage of the beneficiary. On the other hand, an annuity, unlike a liferent (below), need not be limited to the lifetime of a human being. It could be granted for a longer period or it could even be perpetual, such as the endowment of a prize fund. Nowadays, such an endowment would more likely be provided by an initial capital sum which trustees would invest and use the fluctuating interest to fund the particular purpose.

Assuming that the annuity is granted mortis causa the testator can fix the method by which it is to be paid. However, if he directs that an annuity is to be bought for the beneficiary by way of a lump sum payment to an insurance company, with the result that the beneficiary could sell the annuity in return for a capital sum, this could be an example of a repugnant condition (explained below). Normally the testator will provide that the annuitant is entitled to an annuity of £X *per annum* out of the free annual income of the estate. This means that the payment of the annuity is made without diminishing the capital of the estate. However if, in the future, the income of the trust fund is not sufficient to pay the annuity in full, the trustees must make up the full amount of the annuity by encroaching on the capital (unless the trust deed prohibits this, in which case the annuity would have to be reduced).

Although traditionally an annuity was for a fixed sum, the value of such an income is bound to be eroded by inflation. It is perfectly in order for an annuity provision to be inflation-proofed in some way, but this has to be provided for expressly, not merely by implication.

LIFERENT AND FEE

5–08 It is necessary to distinguish a liferent from an annuity. It has just been demonstrated that, unless provided to the contrary, trustees may encroach on capital (if need be) to pay an annuity in full. The opposite rule applies to a liferent, as (unless the will provides otherwise) no encroachment on capital is permitted. Although liferent can be provided inter vivos it is more commonly provided mortis causa.

A key element of liferent is that there must always be a right of fee, i.e. a full and unencumbered right of property, at the end of the liferent period. So, a common enough provision would be ". . . to my wife Doris in liferent and my son John in fee". If what purports to be a liferent does not have a right of fee at its conclusion, whatever else it may be, it is not a liferent.

The liferenter has the right to use the property and enjoy the income and fruits from it *salva substantia* (without destruction of the substance). It is sometimes necessary to make a fine distinction between income and capital. In the case of an estate of timber, the rule appears to be that the liferenter is entitled to ordinary windfalls, to copse-wood cut in normal course and to wood cut for estate purposes such as fencing. The fiar (person entitled to the fee) is entitled to final mature trees and to trees blown down by extraordinary storms. The liferenter is entitled to royalties from mineral workings let or worked during the lifetime of the testator. Royalties from minerals let or worked after the testator's death normally fall into capital. The liferenter is entitled to dividends from shares and to other cash payments made by the company out of profits. Bonus shares are classed as capital unless they are issued in lieu of a cash dividend. Most liferents set up by a will are said to be "beneficiary" (sometimes called "improper") which means that the property is held by trustees during the liferent period.

At the end of the liferent, the trustees "denude" in favour of the fiar.

The Apportionment Act 1870 provides that all rents, regular annual receipts, dividends and interest are to be considered as accruing from day to day. This means in practice that the liferenter is only entitled to income on the trust investments which actually accrue during the liferent period. So, income accrued before the commencement of the liferent period (usually the date of the testator's death) falls ("effeirs") to capital, as does income accrued after its termination. If shares are bought during the liferent, the liferenter receives only the proportion of dividend accrued after purchase. Similarly, if shares are sold, the liferenter only receives the proportion of income accrued up to date of sale. Clearly, this is all rather complicated. It is perfectly competent, and invariable professional practice, to disapply the provisions of the Act in the testamentary deed.

The crucial concept to grasp is that the fiar actually owns the property but cannot enjoy the fee absolute (ownership *and* possession) until the burden of the liferent comes to an end.

Traditionally, liferents tended to affect heritable property but, with the passage of time, liferents of both heritable and moveable property have become more common. A classic situation would be where a testator directs that his house is to be held by his trustees in liferent to his widow until her death or remarriage and then to the child(ren) in fee. The effect of this provision is that the widow may continue to live in the house without it ever becoming her property.

One obvious good reason for such a provision is to prevent the house going out of the family, should the liferenter remarry. Although a fiar does acquire a vested right in the property at the time of the testator's death (*a morte testatoris*), actual possession of the subjects is not given until the termination of the liferent. To put it another way, the liferenter's right is a burden on the fiar's right to the property so that although the fiar could sell the property during the subsistence of the liferent, he cannot give a higher or better right than he himself possesses. Thus any purchaser or secured creditor can only take the property subject to the rights of the liferenter.

As indicated above, liferent includes the rights to enjoy the fruits or income from property without diminishing the capital. So if (as is often the case) the liferented property is a house, the liferenter (to use the example quoted above) would bear the expense of the upkeep of the property, plus the usual burdens such as local taxes, insurance and normal maintenance (an elusive concept at the best of times) of the property. The liferenter would also pay any interest on a heritable security, but would not be liable to repay any of the capital of an outstanding mortgage. Larger repairs or more fundamental alterations or renovations would probably be the responsibility of the fiar but each instance would have to be considered on its merits. In practice, parties may come to their own arrangements about who pays for what.

If the liferenter were to leave the property for good, it would revert to the fiar in fee absolute.

Alimentary liferents

5–09 Sometimes a liferent is declared in the will to be alimentary, with the intention of providing for the maintenance of the liferenter. Traditionally, a liferent was declared to be alimentary in order to provide the liferenter with some safeguard against personal rashness and to give some protection against hard times. It would be of most relevance where the property includes more than a dwelling house, such as an element of income.

The are two main features of an alimentary liferent. First, it may not be assigned, e.g. by sale, gift or security, to a third party. The alimentary liferent is entirely personal to the liferenter. Once it has been accepted, it cannot be assigned or renounced. Secondly, it is not liable to the diligence of creditors. This means that the liferent funds may not be arrested in the hands of the trustees, as third parties. It should, however, be noted that it is only protected to the extent that the income payable to the liferenter is reasonable, bearing in mind the liferenter's own personal circumstances and position in life. Any excess over such a reasonable amount will be liable to diligence. What is reasonable is always a matter of fact.

There are cases where a beneficiary has wished to assign or renounce the liferent. At common law, an alimentary liferent cannot be revoked once it has become operational. It can, however, be revoked *before* it becomes operational (*Douglas-Hamilton v Hamilton's Trustees*, 1961 S.C. 205). Under s.1 of the Trusts (Scotland) Act 1961, the court may allow an arrangement to vary or revoke an alimentary liferent provided it is satisfied that such an arrangement is reasonable in the circumstances, e.g. that there is sufficient income from other sources for the maintenance of the liferenter. Normally an alimentary liferent is expressly declared by the testator to be alimentary, but this is not actually essential. Provided the testator makes it clear in some other words that the liferent is of an alimentary nature, this is sufficient in law to give it that status.

Right of occupancy

5–10 It is necessary to distinguish a right of liferent from a right of occupancy of a dwellinghouse. The latter right is a lesser right than that of liferent; it merely confers a personal right to occupy the subjects stated for a specific period, as directed. An occupant would be liable for local taxes, but not for the type of repairs normally carried out by a landlord nor for interest on a heritable security. Sometimes there may be a problem in deciding whether the testator has, in fact, granted a right of occupancy or a liferent. In the case of *Cathcart's Trustees v Allardice* (1900) 2 F. 326, it was held that even though the word "liferent" had been used in a will, only a right to occupy had been intended.

RESIDUARY AND SUBSTITUTIONARY PROVISIONS

In the course of human history, many people have claimed to be able to see into the future. Readers can make their own assessments of such claims. In dealing with succession, while it is not necessary to attempt to foretell the future, it is necessary to consider at least a range of viable possibilities as to what eventualities could take place in the future. **5–11**

The residue clause

It is fair to assume that if a person makes a will, the intention is that this document will deal with the whole of his estate. It would be both perverse and unwise to want to leave a will which only disposes of part of the estate and leaves the rest to intestate succession. Few people, if any, would purposely set out to achieve such an inconvenient mess being made of their affairs after their death. **5–12**

Very few people know exactly how much they are worth in purely financial terms. There is an uncomfortable ring of truth in the cynical saying that most people are "better off dead". Even if a person knows roughly what his house and furniture is worth and how much he has in the bank or building society, it is unlikely that he will be able to take account of every last penny which will be credited to his estate.

One of the many problems of the home made will is that, surprisingly often, a testator will forget altogether about the residue of the estate. Bequests are made of the house and valuables, general legacies to a number of people, but all that is left over is forgotten about. If there has been a long interval between making the will and the death of the testator, the residue could have increased substantially. Equally, it could have diminished. In either case, it is wise to provide properly for the residue.

A typical example of a residue clause would be "I leave the rest, residue and remainder of my means and estate to..." It is common enough, and perfectly in order, for a residuary legatee to be given a special or general legacy in addition to this.

The destination-over

A major purpose of a residue clause is to prevent any part of the estate falling into intestacy. Of course, a problem could arise if the residuary legatee were to die before the testator. The general rule, already explored, is that no one can benefit under a will unless he survives the testator. This seems obvious, since how can anyone benefit if he is dead? However, the question does not so much concern a benefit which the predeceasing legatee did not have the opportunity to enjoy; the real question is, did he, at the time of his death, have what is called a vested right? If he did, that vested right can pass on to his heirs. It is crucially important to understand that a potential beneficiary cannot have a vested right if he dies before the testator. (The wider issue of vesting is explored in Ch.9.) **5–13**

One way of avoiding any legacy failing is to have at least one alternative legatee. This can be achieved by a "whom failing" provision, e.g. the legacy goes ". . . to John, whom failing Betty". The technical name for a "whom failing" provision is a "destination-over". Such a device is simple to insert and common in practice. If John dies before the testator, he has no vested right and the legacy will pass to Betty (assuming, of course, that she does survive the testator).

However, there is another potential problem. Suppose that at the time of the testator's death, John is alive. Obviously, the legacy vests in him. So, where does that leave Betty? Does she have any hope of eventually succeeding to that same legacy when John dies? The simple answer is usually not, but the matter requires further exploration. Unfortunately, it is necessary to look at some technical jargon at this point.

In the destination-over, John is the institute, i.e. the main legatee. Betty is termed either the conditional institute or the substitute. If she is the conditional institute, when John inherits the legacy, Betty's right to inherit is lost; it is sometimes said to "fly off". If, however, Betty is the substitute, there is just a possibility that she could still inherit after John's death. It all depends on what John does during the time of his ownership. If he alienates the legacy by sale or gift, or if he leaves it in his will to someone other than Betty, any right she might have had in it is effectively defeated. But if he does not take any such steps, she could claim it on his death.

Obviously, the crucial question is whether Betty is a conditional institute or a substitute. The first place to look is the actual will itself in the hope that the testator's intentions are clear. If the will is unclear, or is silent, certain legal presumptions will be invoked. Prior to the passing of the 2016 Act, a distinction was made in this regard between heritable and moveable property. If the subject of the legacy was heritable, Betty would be a substitute (*Watson v Giffen* (1884) 11 R. 444). If moveable, she would merely be a conditional institute (*Crumpton's Judicial Factor v Barnardo's Homes*, 1917 S.C. 713). The 2016 Act harmonised the position; under s.8, the second-named legatee is always presumed to be a conditional institute, regardless of whether the subject is heritable or moveable. This is, however, merely a presumption and can be defeated if the will states otherwise, or if the testator's intention can clearly be inferred. Anyone drawing up such a clause would be well-advised to ensure that the testator's wishes are explicitly stated.

VOID CONDITIONS

5–14 It was stated at the beginning of this chapter that, generally, a testator can do as he pleases in his will (subject, always, to legal rights). Whilst this is true, there can be cases where conditions attached to a legacy are seen as being objectionable and so are not given effect.

Impossibility, illegality, immorality or provisions contrary to public policy

A condition may be void if it is impossible, illegal, immoral or contrary to public policy. A condition deemed to be void is said to be *pro non scripto* (treated as not having been written), meaning that the condition is ignored but the actual legacy does not fall, provided it can still logically be given effect. Whilst impossibility and illegality tend to be fairly easy to determine, there is an obvious difficulty in knowing what, in today's diverse society, counts as immoral. What is contrary to public policy may be even more elusive. **5–15**

In *Fraser v Rose* (1849) 11 D. 1466, a daughter was left a legacy by her father on condition that she did not live with her mother (the deceased's widow) who was to be thrown out of the house. The court set aside the condition and the daughter received the legacy unconditionally. Similarly, in the English case of *Re Johnson's Will Trusts* [1967] 1 All E.R. 553, a condition attached to a legacy which could be seen as an encouragement to a wife to leave her spouse was declared to be ineffectual. On the other hand, in *Earl of Caithness v Sinclair*, 1912 S.C. 79, it was not contrary to public policy to make a legacy conditional on the beneficiary not succeeding to a peerage. Nor was it contrary to public policy to require a legatee to cease association with an orphan of whom the testator did not approve (*Balfour's Trustees v Johnston*, 1936 S.C. 137).

Sometimes there is no identifiable beneficiary and, in this case, if the conditions are "objectionable", the entire legacy will fall. Some eccentric testators have attempted to do some rather remarkable things. In *Aitken's Trustees v Aitken*, 1927 S.C. 374, a Musselburgh butcher directed that his shop was to be demolished and, on its site, was to be erected a massive bronze statue of himself. This legacy was struck down; to put it in non-legal language, the provision was "over the top". Expressed more conventionally, such provisions have been seen by the court as an abuse of the power of testation.

In *McCaig v University of Glasgow (No.2)*, 1907 S.C. 231, Mr McCaig, who built the famous "folly" overlooking Oban, directed his testamentary trustees to erect artistic towers and statues of himself and his family on his estate. His sister challenged the legacy and the court struck it down as being of no benefit to anyone. Later, in an ironic twist, the same sister attempted to do something similar in her will, which included erecting statues of the McCaig family on top of the "folly". These provisions were also struck down (*McCaig's Trustees v Lismore United Free Kirk Session*, 1915 S.C. 426).

Others provisions that have been struck down include the exhumation of friends' bodies in order that they be interred with the deceased (*Mackintosh's Judicial Factor v Lord Advocate*, 1935 S.C. 406), and money directed to the public displaying of an art collection which was deemed to be of insufficient interest to warrant the cost involved (*Sutherland's Trustee v Verschoyle*, 1968 S.L.T. 43).

It is also possible for a condition or legacy to fail because of uncertainty. This issue is considered in Ch.7.

Repugnancy

5–16 A legacy is said to have a repugnant condition if that condition is inconsistent with the main tenor of the legacy itself. One example would be where a legacy appears to be given absolutely and without restriction, but trustees are then directed to hold the capital and pay only the revenue to the beneficiary. In such a case, the direction to the trustees to hold the capital would be repugnant and the beneficiary would receive payment of the capital of his legacy. Another possible example would be where a testator directs that an annuity be purchased for the legatee, as in *Dow v Kilgour's Trustees* (1877) 4 R. 403, but the legatee could immediately sell the annuity for a lump sum. In such a case, the beneficiary would be entitled to payment of the lump sum which would have been used to buy the annuity. In *Miller's Trustees v Miller* (1890) 18 R. 301, a father left property in trust for his son. The trustees of the estate were directed to administer the property until he attained the age of 25, or on his earlier marriage, at which date he would attain a full vested right. The son married before the age of 25 but his father's trustees refused to denude in his favour. It was held that where an absolute right of property is given to a beneficiary of full age, he can require the trustees to denude in his favour, even if the original will had directed retention for a longer period. If there had been other trust purposes still to be carried out, or if the trustees had been given some element of discretion, the son would not have been able to make the trustees denude until he attained the age of 25.

Accumulation of income

5–17 Although now contained in later statute, the law originated in the Accumulations Act 1800, better known as the Thelluson Act. In *Thellusson v Woodford* (1799) 4 Ves. Jr. 227; (1805) 11 Ves. 112, a very wealthy English merchant directed that his entire estate was to be invested in land and the income accumulated. His estate was only to be shared out among members of his family when the last of the class of his children and/or grandchildren died. In other words, he was effectively passing over two generations. In Scotland, his children could at least have claimed legal rights but not so south of the border. When the case came to the House of Lords, it was decided, with reluctance, that the provisions of the will were valid. The 1800 Act was passed as a knee-jerk reaction to ensure that history did not repeat itself. The current law is found in the Trusts (Scotland) Act 1961 and the Law Reform (Miscellaneous Provisions) (Scotland) Act 1966, although they are still referred to as the Thelluson Act provisions. It is not possible to contract out of these statutory provisions. There are actually six possible maximum periods of accumulation, explained in more detailed and specialised textbooks.

As far as testamentary trustees are concerned, the simple rule of thumb is that income cannot be accumulated for more than 21 years from the death of the testator. Income directed to be accumulated contrary to the statutory provisions goes to those who would have otherwise been entitled to it, i.e. if accumulation had not been directed in the first place. It is perfectly legal to accumulate for up to 21 years, and whatever fund is thus "in the bag" is perfectly legitimate, but after the 21 years have passed, the surplus income must be distributed even if the original will or trust disposition and settlement provide otherwise.

One leading case is *Elder's Trustees v Free Church of Scotland* (1892) 20 R. 2. Mr Elder provided in his will for an adequate annuity for his widow, but the whole residue of his estate was to be held by trustees until her death. On Mrs Elder's death, the trustees were to set aside certain legacies to provide a Chair in one of the Free Church Colleges, to erect and endow a new Free Church, with a manse, and to apply any remaining estate to schemes of the Free Church to be selected by his trustees. The income from the estate more than covered Mrs Elder's annuity and surplus income was accumulated. She survived her husband by more than 21 years, so further accumulation thereafter was void. The question arose as to who was entitled to this surplus revenue. Not surprisingly, the Free Church of Scotland claimed to be the residuary legatee and thus entitled to the revenue. However, the church was not the residuary legatee. The residue was to be paid to schemes of the church to be selected by the trustees and this selection could only take place after Mrs Elder died. So, until Mrs Elder died, there could be no residuary legatee. Accordingly, the surplus revenue fell into intestate succession.

It would seem it is not possible for legal rights to be claimed out of such revenue. Although this has been permitted in some historic cases, the stance most recently taken is that as such revenue comes into the estate after the death of the testator, legal rights cannot be claimed against it because, as mentioned in Ch.3, these are fixed at the moment of death (*Lindsay's Trustees v Lindsay*, 1931 S.C. 586).

Creation of certain liferents

The Law Reform (Miscellaneous Provisions) (Scotland) Act 1968 s.18 **5–18**
provides that it is not possible to create a liferent in favour of someone who is not alive or *in utero* (in the womb) at the date of the creator's death. If someone tries to do this, the effect is that the liferent property belongs absolutely to the beneficiary at the date when hebecomes entitled to the liferent, provided he is aged 18. If the beneficiary is younger, he must wait until attaining the age of 18.

TESTAMENTARY PROVISIONS AND LEGAL RIGHTS

It has been remarked several times that legal rights cannot be defeated by a **5–19**
will. This is because the law imposes certain responsibilities to provide for one's immediate family. In life, these responsibilities are reflected by the obligation to financially support one's spouse (or civil partner) and children. In death, they are reflected by legal rights.

The theory of legal rights in testacy is simple enough; any person entitled to claim legal rights may do so, regardless of a will's contents. However, the claimant must elect between such rights and any legacy in his favour; he cannot have both. This legal principle is named "approbate and reprobate" which, in simple terms, means that it is not possible for someone both to accept and reject the same document. Put more colloquially, a claimant cannot "have his cake and eat it too".

Rejecting the legacy

5–20 In a testate estate, the executor (or solicitor acting for him) would normally intimate a legacy to the person entitled to it. If the beneficiary decides to instead claim legal rights, he would normally be required to put both the claim and the renunciation of the legacy in writing; however, there is no statutory style prescribed. Sometimes members of a family may be reluctant to claim legal rights rather than a legacy, in the mistaken belief that it will require some kind of court action and that, in some way, the will may have to be contested. There is much scope for misunderstanding in this area and it merely underlines how important it is for members of a family to seek competent advice on an individual basis.

Indeed, it should be stressed that claiming legal rights rather than a legacy does not create intestacy. However, an uncommon but important exception is where the rejected legacy is the only provision in the will. This was the situation in the memorable case of *Kerr, Petitioner*, 1968 S.L.T. (Sh. Ct) 61, which demonstrated that sometimes a surviving spouse could be better off under intestacy than being left everything under the deceased's will. In *Kerr*, a widow was left all of her husband's relatively modest estate. There were no other bequests under the will. The children of the marriage wished to claim their legal rights. If they were to succeed, obviously less of the estate would be available to the widow. If the husband had died intestate, however, the widow's prior rights would have exhausted the entire estate. The widow decided to disclaim her benefit under the will and, as her legacy was the only provision, the estate fell into intestacy. She then claimed her prior rights and received the entire estate. The children could still, as a matter of law, claim legal rights, but as there were no remaining funds to meet them, these rights were worth precisely nothing.

Accepting the legacy

5–21 Unless there is express provision to the contrary, in all wills made after the 1964 Act came into force, any provision in favour of spouses, civil partners or children is deemed to be in full and final settlement of legal rights. It does not matter whether the legacy provision is of heritable or moveable property or both, nor whether the provision is more or less generous than legal rights; the same principle applies. In effect, accepting a legacy provision, by statutory implication, serves as a renunciation of legal rights after the death of the parent. Thus if there are two children and each is left property in the parent's will but one elects to take legal rights, he receives only one half of the notional legitim fund. It is possible for a will to provide that a beneficiary will not lose his right to claim legal rights by accepting a legacy but such a provision is uncommon.

Legal rights in testate succession example

Phil E. Buster, a retired politician, has died. He is survived by his wife Bertha **5–22**
and two children, Billy and Brenda. Phil's net estate is £369,500, comprising the family home (worth £320,000), an antique sceptre (£16,000), a portrait of Phil's favourite former Prime Minister (£500) and other moveable property valued at £33,000. In his will, Phil has directed that his entire estate be given over to a fund that supports retired Parliamentarians, which his family are very unhappy about. Having been advised that Phil's will is valid and that there was no question regarding his mental capacity at the time of drafting, the family's only option is to claim legal rights.

If they do so, the net moveable estate must be calculated and divided as it would upon intestacy. The sceptre, portrait and other moveables together are worth £49,500 (the house, which is heritable, is not counted). Bertha can claim one third of this amount, so she will receive £16,500. Billy and Brenda will share another one third between them and will receive £8,250 each. The remaining one third of the moveable estate, plus the house, will be distributed according to the terms of the will; therefore the retired Parliamentarians' fund will receive £16,500 moveables plus the £320,000 of heritables, for a total of £336,500.

It is not difficult to see that the family of a testator who left such a will might feel aggrieved at how they have been treated. Whilst these feelings might be justified from a moral perspective, from a legal point of view the position is clear and there is little (if anything) else that the family could do. Perhaps the best advice would be to ensure that family relations are kept so amicable as to prevent a testator wishing to disinherit his family in the first place!

6. ALTERATIONS AND ADDITIONS

6–01 After someone has made a will, it is common and sensible practice for him to leave it with his law agent for safekeeping. It is certainly possible, even probable, that at some future date the testator may wish to make amendments to his will. Alternatively he may make entirely new provisions, particularly if circumstances change, e.g. if a main beneficiary were to die before the testator. Opportunities should be taken, at appropriate times, to update and review the settlement. Even today, many people are surprisingly resistant to making new wills, but this resistance may well disadvantage their family members or other legatees.

Existing wills may be altered or superseded in a number of different ways, which will now be examined separately.

CODICIL

6–02 A codicil is a short deed granted by a testator making alterations to an original will. It is particularly useful where the original will is long and complicated, though perhaps in the digital age it might be as easy to retrieve an electronic copy of an existing will, make minor alterations and have the entire updated document signed of new.

A codicil could be used, for example, to increase a general legacy to keep pace with inflation or to add a new grandchild to the list of beneficiaries. Sometimes a will may have several codicils. The tradition, in the days of writing or typewriting, was to engross the codicil onto the main will or, alternatively, to stitch it in as an appendix. It can just as easily be an entirely separate document, which is more likely these days, but care should be taken to keep both documents together. If it is a true codicil, it will be quite clear that both the original will and the codicil(s) are to be read as one and that they are not two or more separate wills. In other words, the codicil should specifically refer to the original will and confirm the parts which are not expressly revoked.

A simple example of a codicil would be as follows:

I, JENNY BROWN, designed in the foregoing Will dated the Sixth day of February Nineteen Hundred and Ninety seven (hereinafter referred to as "my Will"), being desirous of making certain alterations and additions thereto, Do Hereby (First) increase the legacy to William Smith, designed in Clause Third of my Will to Ten Thousand pounds (£10,000); (Second) direct my executor to pay, as soon as convenient after my death but without interest to the date of payment, the sum of Five Thousand pounds (£5,000) to my housekeeper and companion, Mrs Euphemia Muckle, Eight Low Street, Aberfeldy. And except in so far as amended by this Codicil, I confirm my Will in all respects (*To be attested)*

REVOCATION OF A PREVIOUS WILL

When a person makes an entirely new will, it is important to revoke all prior testamentary documents so that there is no doubt as to what the testator's true intentions actually were. Having more than one operative will in place is ill-advised and unnecessarily confusing, although as discussed below the situation is not unheard of. **6–03**

Revocation can be carried out in a number of ways.

Revocation by physical destruction

The testator, if he wishes to revoke the entire will, may destroy the deed by completely tearing it up (or shredding it), either in person or by giving express authority to his law agent or some other person. This revokes the will, assuming that the testator possessed the *animus revocandi* (intention to revoke). If the destruction was accidental, or carried out during a period where the testator lacked mental capacity, it may not finally revoke the will. Although a complicated situation, it is possible for a court action to be raised to "prove the tenor" (content) of the document. Good evidence of the contents of a missing will would be a copy or draft, but reliable witness evidence may also be sufficient (*Leckie v Leckie* (1884) 11 R. 1088). **6–04**

It is important to note one presumption applied by the courts. If it can be shown that a testator executed a will and that, thereafter, he retained that will in his own custody but at the time of his death it cannot be found, there is the presumption that he completely destroyed it *animo revocandi* (with the intention to revoke). Like most presumptions, it can be rebutted, but the burden of the proof is on the party who seeks to do so (*Laing v Bruce* (1838) 1 D. 59). In *Clyde v Clyde*, 1958 S.C. 343, a testator made a will, favouring his nephew, and left the document with his solicitors. Some considerable time later (and several years before his eventual death) he requested his solicitor to send the will to him. At the time of his death, the will could not be found and it was held to have been intentionally destroyed by the testator.

Occasionally, it is possible to encounter examples of what can only be described as partial destruction. What if there is a will but parts of the text have been scored out or obliterated? It is obvious that this could easily have been done fraudulently, so there would need to be some evidence that the obliteration was carried out by the testator (or with the testator's express authority) and not by some unscrupulous third party.

Normally, the court would require some form of authentication of the deletion, such as initials, signature or written explanation. In each case, the court would also require to look at all the relevant facts and circumstances. In *Thomson's Trustees v Bowhill Baptist Church*, 1956 S.L.T. 302, certain clauses in a will had been scored out, then physically cut out with scissors, the testator had signed near the gap and signed a written explanation above and below the gaps. In the circumstances, it was held that the missing clauses had been validly deleted.

Revocation by later will

6–05 A common method of revocation is an express declaration in a later will that earlier wills are "hereby revoked". Generally speaking, a declaration of this kind is effective. If there is no express revocation and the earlier will has not been destroyed in a regular manner, it may be that the two wills have to be read together. Of course, it is unlikely that this is what the testator would have wished, unless he perceived his second will as being in the nature of an extended codicil, in which case that fact ought to have been made clear.

In some cases, revocation (or partial revocation) may be implied in so far as the earlier will is inconsistent with the later one. A rule of thumb is that if the later will is a universal settlement, the earlier will is revoked by implication (*Cadger v Ronald's Trustees*, 1946 S.L.T. (Notes) 24). However, if the two wills can be read together, the general rule is that they would both be effective. In *Duthie's Executors v Taylor*, 1986 S.L.T. 142, a second will conveyed the testator's whole estate to trustees but made no direction as to the residue of the estate (which had been done in the earlier will). The two wills were read together and most of the legacies in the earlier will were effective.

If it is claimed that a later will revokes an earlier will by implication, it appears that the party alleging such revocation requires to discharge a very heavy burden of proof. In *Mitchell's Administratrix v Edinburgh Royal Infirmary*, 1928 S.C. 47, a codicil to a will was ambivalent on the matter of revocation of certain provisions made in the principal will. The evidence led in attempting to ascertain the testator's intention was inconsistent; the court held that the burden had not been satisfied and the original provisions stood.

Revocation by the *conditio si testator sine liberis decesserit*

6–06 The *conditio si testator* is an ancient common law presumption that where a testator makes a universal settlement, e.g. "my whole means and estate to. . .", that will is revoked by the subsequent birth of a child to the testator. The presumption raised by the *conditio* is based on the notion that the testator would not have wished such a will to stand where it made no provision for the child or children. The presumption could be rebutted by circumstances which show that the testator intended that the will should stand, e.g. by making suitable inter vivos provisions for the child (*Stuart-Gordon v Stuart-Gordon* (1899) 1 F. 1005).

The *conditio* does not operate automatically and must be invoked by the later-born child. This is not the same as a legal rights claim, and successfully invoking the *conditio* will totally revoke the will. As a result, the estate will fall into intestacy. If this happens, prior rights would be claimable, and there is the risk that the entire estate could be exhausted before the child can benefit; if this is likely to be the case, the child may be better off simply claiming legal rights instead.

The modern relevance of the *conditio si testator* has been questioned, although it was successfully invoked in a somewhat recent case (*Greenan v Courtney* [2007] CSOH 58). The Scottish Law Commission has recommended that the *conditio* be abolished, however at the time of writing this has not occurred.

Revival of a revoked will

A question may arise as to whether a revoked will can later be revived. The general rule under common law was that if a subsequent will was itself revoked, the earlier will would revive as if the later had never existed. **6–07**

However, such situations could be very complicated and the case law was inconsistent. Express revocation by a second will coupled with destruction of the first would make revival less likely. But where the first will had not been destroyed it would be more likely to revive. A useful illustration is provided by *Bruce's Judicial Factor v Lord Advocate*, 1969 S.C. 296. In 1945, Mr Bruce signed a will, which remained with his law agents. In 1949, he signed a second will, revoking all previous wills, but he retained this second will in his possession. At the time of his death, the second will could not be found. The court held that Bruce had destroyed the second will *animo revocandi* and, though not without some difficulty, decided that the first will was effective.

Another potential problem could arise whereby a second will is proven to be invalid and an earlier valid will has been revoked and destroyed. What is the status, if any, of the earlier will? In *Cullen's Executor v Elphinstone*, 1948 S.C. 662, such a problem arose. A second will was signed and, in accordance with professional practice, the earlier will was destroyed. It transpired that the second will was not properly executed and was thus invalid. The court held that although the earlier will had certainly been destroyed, it had not been validly revoked. There was sufficient evidence as to its contents and a declarator of tenor was granted.

Due to the uncertainty which plagued this area, clarity has been provided by the 2016 Act. Under s.5, where a will, or any part of it, has been expressly or impliedly revoked by a subsequent will, it shall not be revived by revocation of that subsequent will. In such a situation the estate will fall into intestacy. This reverses the common law position, though its exact effects in practice remain to be seen.

Subsequent divorce or dissolution

A further matter related to revocation is the effect that subsequent divorce of the testator (or dissolution of a civil partnership) has on an existing will. The common law position was that termination of such a relationship did not revoke a will and would not necessarily defeat succession rights. Case decisions were inconsistent, and in practice succession rights were often specifically renounced under a separation agreement, though careful wording was required to ensure this was achieved. In *Price v Baxter*, 2009 Fam. L.R. 138, a husband had made a will leaving his entire estate to his wife. The **6–08** couple separated, and both spouses signed a minute of agreement renouncing any rights of succession arising under statute or common law. When the husband died, the two were still married and his will remained unchanged. The wife successfully claimed the husband's estate, since succession rights *under a will* had not expressly been renounced.

The position was altered by the 2016 Act. Under s.1, divorce or dissolution shall have the effect of treating the former spouse or civil partner as having predeceased the testator in terms of any benefit derived under the will, unless the provision expressly states otherwise. This does not revoke the will itself but ultimately it achieves the same result in respect of the relevant provisions. If the only legacy was in favour of the former spouse or civil partner, then in absence of a destination-over the estate would fall into intestacy.

It should be noted that these provisions apply only in respect of actual divorce or dissolution. Mere separation is not enough, and formal agreements continue to regulate rights whilst the relationship still legally persists. Thus a situation such as that which arose in the *Price* case above would not be affected by the 2016 Act.

MUTUAL WILLS

6–09 Mutual wills are arrangements in which two or more parties sign the same testamentary document. They were historically popular with married couples who wanted to leave wills in identical terms.

A question that has occupied the courts on a few occasions is whether the document is contractual in nature or whether the parties are free to revoke their respective parts of the testamentary provisions. Such revocation might be before or after the death of the other party.

As a very general rule, a mutual will is simply two or more wills run together. Thus the parties are free to revoke all or any of the testamentary provisions made by them individually. If the parties are spouses or civil partners, it is perhaps more likely that the terms of the document will be deemed contractual and so unbreakable. Judicial treatment has, however, been decidedly mixed.

Mutual wills have become increasingly rare in practice and are almost certainly best avoided.

7. INTERPRETATION OF WILLS

In order for a will to be given effect, it must be sufficiently clear what the provisions actually instruct. It has already been observed that there are situations in which a testator's intentions might not be entirely clear. In such difficult cases, questions of interpretation must be addressed. If it cannot be discerned what ought to be done, the will (or certain provisions) may fall, and the estate may be fully or partially intestate. **7–01**

THE GENERAL RULE

This is a complex area in its own right and only the basics can be covered in a book of this size. As a very general rule, if a court is called upon to interpret a will, it does so intrinsically, i.e. within the four corners of the document. The question, in other words, is "What does the will actually say?" This may well be different from what beneficiaries or potential beneficiaries might wish it to say. **7–02**

EXTRINSIC EVIDENCE

Extrinsic evidence, i.e. evidence from outside the four corners of the deed, will not generally be permitted when it comes to ascertaining the intention of the testator. Where the testator's words are perfectly clear, it is not competent to lead evidence that the testator actually had a different intention. It is perhaps obvious that if such evidence were permitted, the system could be open to abuse by disappointed prospective beneficiaries trying to stake a claim. A testator is presumed to use words in their normal manner, unless the context shows otherwise. In *Yule's Trustees, Petitioners,* 1981 S.L.T. 250, "child" was interpreted as meaning a grandchild in the particular context. **7–03**

Having said all that, there are times when the court will allow extrinsic evidence. If the will is written in a foreign language or in some form of code, external evidence by way of translation is permitted, which is no more than common sense. More problematic situations include: where it is claimed that the will had been signed under facility and circumvention or undue influence; where the will had not been properly executed; or even allegations that the will is a forgery. If extrinsic evidence could not be brought forward in such cases, there would be no possible means of challenge; this would not, of course, be satisfactory.

There may also be cases (and this is where it becomes rather more technical) where extrinsic evidence may be allowed to clarify what was *known* to the testator at the time he signed the will. This is a very different matter from attempting to show that the testator actually meant something different from what he expressly said. In *Dunsmure v Dunsmure* (1879) 7

R. 261, a testator made a legacy of "any money I am entitled to by my father's will, or any other will". The testator was also due money under his parents' marriage contract. In the circumstances, the court concluded that the testator's intention was to bequeath any property due to him under any settlement having the same effect as a will and accordingly held that these funds should also be included under the legacy.

Among the range of factors that need to be clear to a testator are whom he intended to benefit and which property he had in mind. In such cases, minor errors in description need not be fatal and the true facts could allow for extrinsic evidence being introduced.

Two related cases considered questions regarding the legacy's object. In *Wedderspoon v Thomson's Trustees* (1824) 3 S. 396, Thomson had left £500 to "Janet Keiller or Williamson, confectioner in Dundee". There was no such person. The legacy was successfully claimed by an Agnes Keiller (or Wedderspoon), who was married to a confectioner in Dundee. The court was satisfied, by extrinsic evidence, that only a clerical error was involved. In *Keiller v Thomson's Trustees* (1826) 4 S. 724, the same Thomson had left a legacy to "William Keiller, confectioner in Dundee". Again, there was no such person. There were, however, two possible claimants: William Keiller, confectioner in Montrose and James Keiller, confectioner in Dundee. The court considered extrinsic evidence and decided that the testator had intended the legacy to go to James Keiller of Dundee.

Similar rules will apply if the subject of the legacy is in doubt, e.g. if a testator owns two houses in Glebe Street, Anyburgh and he bequeaths "my house in Glebe Street, Anyburgh", which one is intended? If it is not clear from the will, the court will consider extrinsic evidence. However, it will not do so lightly and certainly not if the provision can be made sense of in itself. In *Fortunato's Judicial Factor v Fortunato*, 1981 S.L.T. 277, a legatee sought to lead extrinsic evidence that a public house she had been bequeathed should also include the dwelling above it; the court did not accept this since the will was sufficiently clear.

If the identity of the legatee or the subject matter is still in doubt after leading extrinsic evidence, the legacy will be of no effect. In cases of doubt, the court will, if possible, interpret the provision in a way that avoids total or partial intestacy. In *Magistrates of Dundee v Morris* (1858) 3 Macq. 134, testamentary trustees were directed to set up a school, but no actual cash sum was stated. However, as the will did specify the size of the proposed school, the amount of the legacy required could be ascertained and the provision did not fail from uncertainty.

LEGACIES TO FAMILY MEMBERS

7–04 The object of a legacy is usually identifiable without difficulty and, as shown above, minor errors are not normally fatal. Potential problems can arise, however, with legacies left to relations who are referred to by designation rather than (or in addition to) by name. In *Robertson's Judicial Factor v*

Robertson, 1968 S.L.T. 32, a legacy to "dependants" failed due to the uncertainty of that word. In most cases, a legacy to "next-of-kin" means to those who would have been entitled under intestacy, unless the will bears otherwise, but would not include representatives. However, a bequest to "heirs" would include next-of-kin and representatives.

At common law, a "child" meant only legitimate offspring unless the context clearly indicated otherwise. As outlined in Ch.3, various legislative developments mean that the term is now presumed to include adopted and illegitimate children; wills executed before the relevant statutory provisions came into force are not subject to these presumptions. Also at common law, "full age" was the traditional 21 years, but this was lowered to 18 under the Age of Majority (Scotland) Act 1969. "Issue" includes children as well as direct descendants, such as grandchildren or great grandchildren, who can represent a predeceasing parent or ancestor or claim their vested right.

Problems can also arise with use of words such as "husband" and "wife". Under common law, divorce had no effect on provisions under a will, so in *Couper's Judicial Factor v Valentine*, 1976 S.L.T. 83, a legacy to "my wife, Dorothy Couper" was valid despite the two having been divorced before the testator's death. As observed in Ch.6, under the 2016 Act divorce or dissolution will result in the beneficiary being treated as having pre-deceased. Whilst this certainly addresses the most common problem with such situations, it does not accommodate all peculiarities. In *Burns' Trustees, Petitioners*, 1961 S.C. 17, a provision to "my nephew and his wife and children" was successfully claimed by a *second* wife of the nephew, who had divorced and remarried. The precisely-worded provisions of the 2016 Act would have no effect on such a legacy and so would not change the result if a similar situation arose.

CUMULATIVE AND SUBSTITUTIONAL LEGACIES

In cases where a will (or wills) provides two or more legacies to the same person, the question could arise as to whether these provisions are intended to be cumulative, i.e. all of them payable, or substitutional, i.e. one taking the place of the other. Obviously, the first place to look for guidance is the actual will itself. If there is no guidance, a number of presumptions will apply. **7–05**

If the legacies are contained in the same document and are for the same amount, it is presumed that the testator (and presumably his law agent!) did this in a moment of absent mindedness. In such a case the provisions are substitutional. In all other cases they are presumed to be cumulative. Illogical as it may be, it was held in *Gillies v Glasgow Royal Infirmary*, 1960 S.C. 438 that where there are two identical provisions of a share of residue, these were nevertheless cumulative.

Occasionally, a testator may leave two wills, both of which are valid. Provided both of these wills are valid, all provisions—whether identical or not—are cumulative, as shown in the case of *Arres' Trustees v Mather* (1881) 9 R. 107. Fortunately, this problem does not often arise.

PRECATORY BEQUESTS

7–06 Occasionally, a problem can arise when the testator does not indicate clearly whether he is merely expressing a wish or giving an actual instruction. Such an expression of wish is known as a precatory bequest, from the Latin *precari* (to pray). The problem might arise most frequently in a home-made will, where a testator is more likely to use words such as "would like" or "prefer" rather than more assertive verbs such as "instruct" or "direct" found in professionally drafted wills. The obvious question is whether or not such a precatory provision is binding in law, apart from any possible moral obligation. The rough rule of thumb seems to be that if a wish is expressed to an executor or testamentary trustee, it is more likely to be taken as an instruction than if it is expressed to a beneficiary. Thus in *Barclay's Executor v M'Leod* (1880) 7 R. 477, a desire expressed to an inheriting spouse that she should make testamentary provisions for other relatives was not legally binding. On the other hand, in *Reid's Trustees v Dawson*, 1915 S.C. (HL) 47, where a testator "preferred" his trustees to pay a capital sum to a beneficiary, this was held to be an instruction and thus a valid bequest. There may also be cases where a request or instruction to an executor cannot be carried out. In *Milne v Smith*, 1982 S.L.T. 129, the testator provided a legacy to his son in the hope that the partnership, of which the father had been part, would be continued by the son. This was beyond the powers of the executor to fulfil and the legacy was paid without being subject to conditions.

DISPOSITIVE DISCRETION

7–07 It is not unusual for a testator to give his executors or testamentary trustees some degree of dispositive discretion, meaning that they have discretion, within certain parameters, as to who might benefit and/or by how much. Thus a testator might provide a sum of money to be divided among "such charitable organisations favouring orphaned children as my trustees, in their absolute discretion, may select". In such a case, the general intention of the testator is perfectly clear since a class of beneficiaries is identified.

However, a testator cannot entirely delegate his power to test. If the discretion is completely open-ended, the bequest may fail from uncertainty. In *Anderson v Smoke* (1898) 25 R. 493, there was a direction to trustees to dispose of the residue of the estate in any way they should think fit; this provision was void from uncertainty. There is a considerable body of case law on the legal viability of such phrases as "public, religious, educational and charitable purposes" which is beyond the realistic scope of this book.

Dispositive discretion cannot be exercised by an executor-dative, even if appointed to a testate estate. In *Angus' Executrix v Batchan's Trustees*, 1949 S.C. 335, a lady left a home-made will which provided for the residue of the estate to be given to "charities". The will failed to appoint an executor. It was held that an executor-dative does not have dispositive discretion and the bequest to charities failed from uncertainty. Had the will appointed an executor, the direction would almost certainly have been valid.

Similar rules would apply where the court has appointed a judicial factor (a person with responsibility to care for an estate). In *Robbie's Judicial Factor v Macrae* (1893) 20 R. 358, the deceased had directed her executors to pay the residue of her estate to such charities as they thought proper within a stated class of charities. On the face of it, this direction was both valid and sensible. Unfortunately, all of her executors died before exercising the discretion and a judicial factor was appointed by the court. It was held that the discretion could not be exercised by a judicial factor.

8. WILL SUBSTITUTES

8–01 Reference has been made in previous chapters to mechanisms that provide an alternative means of disposing of an estate upon death. These are worthy of discussion beyond a passing mention since some, in particular the "special destination", have become an everyday part of legal practice. Others are outlined for sake of completeness and historical interest.

SPECIAL DESTINATIONS

8–02 In Ch.5, consideration was given to what is meant by a destination-over of a legacy. The special destination is rather different. At its simplest, a special destination (or survivorship destination) is where property is held in common by two or more living parties "in joint names and the survivor". Although not a testamentary provision, such an arrangement has testamentary effect in that ownership passes to the survivor upon the death of the other party.

Historically, this device was developed in order to circumvent a rule of Scots law that it was not generally possible to dispose of heritable property by testamentary provision. Despite this rule being abolished under s.20 of the Titles to Land (Consolidation) Act 1868, the popularity of the special destination did not diminish and indeed increased into modern times. Although they can apply to either heritable or moveable property, in practice they are far more commonly encountered in respect of the former.

Any property that passes under a special destination does not form part of the deceased's estate for most purposes, although account is taken of it for inheritance tax. Very occasionally, if a destination is unusually complicated, the executor may be required to complete administrative procedures to convey the property to the beneficiary. In such a case, the value of the property is counted as nil and it is made clear that the executor is only administering it for this limited purpose.

Special destinations have often been the subject of criticism, from both academic and judicial quarters. Indeed, there can be pitfalls in using them. In *Christie's Executrix v Armstrong*, 1996 S.L.T. 948, Mr C and Ms A cohabited in a property in Rutherglen, which they had bought "in joint names and the survivor". Mr C was actually married to another lady, much older than Ms A, and there were children of the marriage. Mr C and Ms A had granted a standard security over the property to a building society, from which they had borrowed the funds to finance the purchase. They had also assigned to the society, in further security, a life insurance policy on Mr C's life and this assignation had been duly intimated to the insurance company. The ink on this documentation was scarcely dry when Mr C died very unexpectedly. The insurance company paid the proceeds of the policy to the building society (which was the correct course). The proceeds were almost identical to the capital sum outstanding and there was a minor capital credit balance of around £30. The title to the house, of course, passed automatically to Ms A, under the special destination. Everyone might have lived happily ever after had Mr C's daughter not, having been appointed as his executor-dative, raised her head above the parapet. She claimed her late father had, in effect, paid off the whole loan and that, as her father's executor, she was entitled to claim repayment of one half of that sum. The action was dismissed since the policy was not part of his estate at the time of his death (because it had been validly assigned to the lender), so he could not be considered as having paid the debt. If the policy had not been assigned in security, the result would have been different; clearly the deceased's estate would only, at the end of the day, have been liable for one half of the outstanding debt.

Despite the potential problems, it remains common practice for legal professionals to insert a special destination into the title of heritable property to be owned by more than one person. It is important to note that property taken in joint names does not in itself constitute nor imply a special destination. It is a point of good practice to suggest that a special destination should only be included where the clients request it, or at least that there should be an explanation of the relevant options so that they may make an informed choice.

The question is bound to arise as to whether or not a special destination can be superseded by a later will. Suppose that title to property was taken in the name of "Terry and June and the survivor". Further suppose that Terry dies, but in his will he leaves his half-share of the property to Beattie. This is a complex area, but the general common law rule is that a later will does not wash out ("evacuate") an existing special destination. It certainly does not do so where the destination is contractual, i.e. where two co-owners have contributed to the cost. If only one party has contributed to the purchase, that party does have power to evacuate the destination but the non-contributing party does not. If the funds were provided by a third party, neither party has the power to evacuate.

In any event, this area has been subject to statutory reform. Under the 1964 Act, a will executed since its commencement cannot evacuate a special destination unless it contains specific reference to the destination *and* a declared intention to evacuate. The rules are strictly applied and special destinations remain the subject of litigation. In *Hill v Hill* [2016] CSOH 10, a married couple owned heritable property in joint names and the survivor. Upon breakdown of the relationship, the wife executed a codicil purporting to revoke the special destination in favour of her son. The court held that she did not have the power to do this and the destination stood.

Also relevant is the effect of divorce or dissolution. At common law, a divorce did not automatically evacuate a special destination any more than it revoked a will. In *Gardner's Executors v Raeburn*, 1996 S.L.T. 745, a couple divorced; the title to their house was in joint names and the survivor. As part of the divorce settlement, the wife conveyed her half share to the husband in return for payment. Unfortunately, the half-share belonging to the husband remained subject to the special destination. When he died, this half share passed to his former wife. This result almost certainly did not reflect the true wishes of the husband. To prevent such a situation arising, it became good practice to ensure that *both* parties conveyed the entire property to the party who was taking the title.

This rule has also been the subject of statutory reform, beginning with the Family Law (Scotland) Act 2006, under which a special destination over heritable property in favour of a spouse or civil partner was rendered ineffective by divorce or dissolution. This was superseded by s.2 of the 2016 Act, which extended the same rule to moveables. The mechanism by which the destination is rendered ineffective is to treat the former spouse or civil partner as having failed to survive the deceased; this is the same method by which legacies are effectively revoked, as seen in Ch.6. In keeping with the provisions regarding legacies, the 2016 Act does permit parties to expressly opt out of the statutory rules.

Also consistent with the provisions regarding legacies is the fact that only divorce or dissolution shall have this effect. Separation of the parties is not enough, however rights can be renounced by formal agreement. In *Redfern's Executors v Redfern*, 1996 S.L.T. 900, spouses signed a separation agreement renouncing any rights of succession in the estate of the other and agreeing to sell their house and share the proceeds. Before the house could be sold, Mr R died. The property was subject to a survivorship destination. It was held that rights of succession (at least in this context) included those normally passing under a special destination. In effect, the separation agreement had evacuated the destination.

Finally, it is important to note that a special destination only operates where one party actually survives the other. As shown in Ch.2, if the parties are killed in a common calamity, neither is presumed to survive the other, unless evidence shows otherwise. Thus the special destination could not operate and each party's share would form part of the relevant estate.

NOMINATIONS

8–03 The deceased may have nominated another party to receive certain funds, such as a bank account or benefits under a pension scheme, on the event of his death. Such a nomination, like a special destination, has a general testamentary effect. A true nomination will be based on a statutory provision, which will require to be checked out in each particular case. In some cases (not many) the funds may still require to be delivered to the executor before payment.

In fact, payments of relatively modest sums to a deceased's next-of-kin are frequently allowed by financial institutions as a matter of privilege, rather than right. If a holder of funds belonging to a deceased person chooses to pay them to anyone other than an executor, he generally does so at his own risk and a confirmed executor would have the right to demand payment again. Usually the maximum value to be paid out under a nomination will be £5,000. The payer will require evidence of death and entitlement. The beneficiary may be required to sign an indemnity, in case an executor appears at a later date.

Generally speaking, a nomination is not evacuated by a subsequent will, although the nomination itself may be revoked by the appropriate statutory documentation. The nomination is invalidated if the nominator subsequently marries or remarries. Similarly to a testamentary provision, if the nominee dies before the nominator, the nomination simply falls.

POLICIES OF INSURANCE

If a policy of life insurance is written under the Married Women's Policies **8–04** of Assurance (Scotland) Act 1880 (as amended), it counts as a separate estate and does not need to be taken into account for the purposes of inheritance tax. The 1880 Act, as amended, applies to both husbands and wives. The spouse who takes out such a policy is counted as a trustee and the beneficiaries have vested rights from the time the policy is taken out. The policy proceeds are payable to the surviving spouse and/or children on production of the death certificate. It is not necessary for the policy to make specific mention of the 1880 Act, provided the creation of the trust is clear.

ANTE-NUPTIAL MARRIAGE CONTRACTS

These somewhat cumbersome arrangements were popular with our **8–05** Victorian forefathers, particularly among the more prosperous classes. In former times, married women were often treated as little better than wayward children when it came to the administration of their own property. A lady of means might have had much to lose if her fortune was entirely at the mercy of her husband.

Shortly before the marriage, the woman transferred her property to trustees but, normally, retained an alimentary liferent in her own favour. Since the consideration of the contract was the marriage taking place, that contract could not come into operation until such time as the marriage was actually solemnised. However, once the contract came into force, it was irrevocable on the grounds that it gave rights to children *nascituri* (yet to be born), unless the contract itself gave express powers of revocation. The law in this area was significantly amended by the Law Reform (Husband and Wife) (Scotland) Act 1984, which abolished many of the rules positioning a wife as inferior to her husband.

Some marriage contracts contain provisions that are clearly intended to be testamentary. It appears to be the case that such provisions are revocable, even if the contract declares them not to be (*Barclay's Trustees v Watson* (1903) 5 F. 926).

DONATIONS MORTIS CAUSA

8–06 Gifts given in contemplation of death are, in themselves, not uncommon, especially when small items of sentimental value are involved. An elderly person may wish to pass such items to members of their family or close friends and this is scarcely controversial. Leaving aside the question of liability to inheritance tax, the question may arise as to whether it counts as an out-and-out gift or a donation mortis causa. If it is an out-and-out gift, it is generally irrevocable. If it is a donation mortis causa, the donor can revoke the donation during his own lifetime. If the recipient predeceases, the donation reverts to the donor. In the case of an insolvent estate, the value of the donation could be reclaimed by the executor or trustee. A donation mortis causa ranks after legal rights but before legacies.

In modern times, the popularity of donations mortis causa significantly reduced, and they have now been virtually abolished by s.25 of the 2016 Act.

REARRANGEMENTS AFTER DEATH

8–07 A final matter worth mentioning here is that beneficiaries under a will may enter into a formal agreement whereby the division of the estate is varied in whatever way they wish. In essence, this agreement serves as a substitute for the deceased's will.

Apart from a special legacy, beneficiaries have a right only to cash, not specific assets. In practice, an executor will frequently come to a private arrangement with beneficiaries as to which specific assets they might wish, such as company shares. No one is obligated to accept any legacy if he does not wish to. He may disclaim a legacy or any right of succession entirely, or he may only take a proportion of his entitlement.

Sometimes there may be tax advantages in completely rearranging the distribution of the estate, and this is the most common motivation being doing so. A written election is required, called a "deed of variation" or "deed of family arrangement". Any election to vary must be made within two years of the deceased's date of death.

A young person aged 16 or 17 can validly renounce legal rights or sign a deed of variation. However, he might raise a subsequent challenge, up to the age of 21, that doing so had caused him substantial prejudice. It would certainly be prudent for an executor to seek judicial ratification of the discharge or variation (under s.4 of the Age of Legal Capacity (Scotland) Act 1991).

9. VESTING AND ACCRETION

It was mentioned in Ch.1 that property law is of great significance to the law of succession. The importance of property classifications, and how this might affect a person's inheritance, has already been discussed. Also of relevance are a number of fundamental principles regarding rights in property, e.g. the clear distinction that exists between the concepts of ownership and possession. These, and certain other related concepts, can lead to a number of problems for the legal practitioner. **9–01**

VESTING OF LEGACIES

In previous chapters, several references have been made to the concept of vesting. If property vests in someone, it is his property. However, it is quite possible to have a vested right in something but not to have possession or full enjoyment of it for a variety of different reasons. A person who is in employment has a vested right to each day of salary which he earns. However, he does not actually receive payment until the appropriate pay day. But should he die during the pay period (say, in the middle of the month), the portion of accrued salary will have vested and would be payable to his estate. **9–02**

It is possible, in fact, for someone to have a vested right in something but not to have the full possession and enjoyment for many years to come. Indeed, it is perfectly possible for someone to die with a vested right, never having enjoyed possession at all. Nevertheless, the question as to whether a right has vested is not merely academic; it is crucial in the matter of succession. It should be obvious that, in a common calamity (discussed in Ch.2), it could be of the utmost importance to determine the order of death.

It is necessary to start with the basics. Until a testator dies, there can be no vested right for a beneficiary. The most the beneficiary can enjoy during the testator's lifetime are expectations. The problem with expectations is that they can be dashed. Thus, even if Aunt Flossie names her nephew Herbert as her sole beneficiary and even if she delivers the will into his hands, he has no vested right. He might die before her, or she could change her mind and execute another will, revoking the one in Herbert's possession. Delivery of a will, even to a beneficiary, does not make it irrevocable. Indeed, even if a will states that its provisions are irrevocable, this statement is of no effect and the testator can still change his mind.

It is only on the death of the testator that rights in succession can actually vest. Indeed, to put this another way, it can be stated quite categorically that the earliest date on which a legacy can vest in a beneficiary is the date of the testator's death. Thus, if there is a clear unconditional bequest, whether general, special or residuary, and the legatee is alive at the time of the testator's death, the legacy vests *a morte testatoris* (from the testator's death). If that legatee subsequently dies before taking possession of the legacy, it will, in turn, pass under his will or his intestacy, as the case may be.

It may be that vesting is postponed for one reason or another. The will should make the position clear. If there is doubt, the general presumption is in favour of early vesting.

But why should vesting ever be postponed? It is easier to answer that question by giving examples:

Example 1. ". . . to my nephew John, provided he survives me by thirty clear days . . ."

Example 2. ". . . to my widow Josephine in liferent and to my son Marmaduke in fee . . ."

Looking at the first example, it is a clear condition of the will that John will not acquire any vested right unless and until he survives the testator by 30 clear days. This kind of provision is increasingly common to prevent a double passing of property in quick succession, as was demonstrated in Ch.2. In this example, the date of vesting is tied to an *uncertain* day. That may sound illogical since such a date can clearly be traced on any calendar by taking the deceased's date of death and adding on 30 days. However, although that date is easily identified, the fact that John will survive for 30 days is not certain. The chances are that he will, but until the uncertainty disappears, there can be no vested right. If he does survive for the 30 days, the uncertainty is removed and on that 30th day he acquires a vested right. This tying to an uncertain day is also sometimes known as a suspensive condition, simply because vesting is suspended until the uncertainty is removed.

The second example perhaps brings a more surprising result, if we look at it from the point of view of Marmaduke. His right is tied to a *certain day*, namely a day that sooner or later *must* arrive. It is not possible to plot it on the calendar, but nevertheless it is certain, because sooner or later the liferent must come to an end. It will end when (not if) one of the following events take place: (1) the liferenter dies, or (2) the liferenter renounces the liferent, or (3) (if the will expressly provides for this) the liferenter remarries.

Marmaduke's right of fee, accordingly, is tied to a certain day, i.e. the end of the liferent. This means that the fee vests in him on the death of his father. Obviously, he does not have possession, but the fee belongs to him, subject to the burden of the liferent. Thus, he can dispose of his right of fee as he wishes, subject always to the rights of the liferenter and, if he predeceases his mother, his right of fee will vest in his heirs. When, eventually, the liferent ends, Marmaduke will enjoy what is called the fee absolute or fee simple, i.e. the fee without any incumbrance of liferent. However, although he will then have full possession, his ownership does not begin at that point, it merely continues.

Among the more problematic legacies in respect of vesting are those where there is some tie to a beneficiary reaching a particular age. As explained above, this is normally counted as a suspensive condition, thus there can be no vesting until the beneficiary attains the stipulated age. However, it is necessary to read the will very carefully as the above rules are actually no more than presumptions where a will is silent on the matter. There is a crucial difference between a legacy vesting *now* in a young person, but being held on his behalf by trustees until he attains, say, the age of 25, and a legacy which gives a particular benefit *provided* the beneficiary survives to age 25, which suspends vesting until that age is attained.

The whole point about vesting is that it gives an element of security to a beneficiary. All the parties (in theory) are aware of their position. It may now come as a surprise to learn that there are cases when even a vested right may be defeated or, in legal jargon, may be subject to defeasance. This is also known as a resolutive condition in a legacy.

Sometimes there may not be complete defeasance, in which case it is said to be partial. An easy example would where John leaves property to his wife Jean in liferent and to "our children" in fee. If there are two children at the time of John's death, they take an immediate vested right in the fee, i.e. half of "the cake". Suppose Jean was pregnant with their third child at the time of her husband's death. When that third child is born, he will acquire an immediate vested right to a share in the fee. This means that the right of the other two children is partly defeated. All three children now have a vested right in one third of the fee.

An example of full defeasance would be where Peter leaves his estate in liferent to his widow Sharon and to their as yet unborn child, whom failing his sister Gertrude. On Peter's death, Gertrude takes an immediate vested right in the fee. If Sharon was pregnant at the time of her husband's death and their child is subsequently born, Gertrude's right of fee is fully defeated.

Vesting is a complex subject in its own right. It can often arise in the context of a destination-over. If the testator directs his trustees to pay a legacy on the occurrence of an event (frequently the testator's death) whom failing to another, obviously the original beneficiary does not take any immediate vested right. So, if the original beneficiary dies before the testator, he cannot acquire any vested right (hopefully, this is now self-evident) and the destination-over takes effect on the death of the testator.

There are cases where the legacy does not vest until a later (uncertain) date; but the same rules will apply, in that survivorship is essential to the acquiring of a vested right. Thus, even if the institute does survive the testator but dies before the time of vesting, the destination-over will operate on the death of the institute and any right will pass to the conditional institute or substitute (and, at this point, the distinction between the two does not matter).

AN EXCEPTION TO THE SURVIVORSHIP RULE IN VESTING

9–03 Having been at great pains to stress the importance of vesting, it is necessary to point out an exception to the general rule about survivorship being of the essence. This is a principle based in common law known as the *conditio si institutus sine liberis decesserit* (better known as the *conditio si institutus*). Although the rule has now been made statutory under s.6 of the 2016 Act, for sake of convenience the common law terminology will be used throughout the following commentary.

Translated, the phrase means "the condition that the institute shall have died without children". It means that, in limited cases, a condition may be read into a bequest that where the institute dies before acquiring a vested right, the institute's children, if they are not provided for in the will, may inherit in preference to other beneficiaries, such as a residuary legatee.

The *conditio si institutus* can only apply where the predeceasing institute is a direct descendant of the testator, and is based on the presumption that, if the testator had foreseen that the institute might die before him, he would have wished the institute's children to take the place of their parent. The *conditio* will not apply if the will indicates expressly or by clear implication that the testator did not intend it to. So, it would not apply where the testator makes express provision for the death of the institute, or where provision is made elsewhere in the will for the institute's descendant.

This kind of situation could not normally arise unless in the context of litigation or by agreement among the family. It would be a rash executor who would take the law into his own hands and apparently bypass another claimant without the authority of the court or a formal writing from the beneficiaries who would lose by the invocation of the *conditio*.

ACCRETION

9–04 Accretion (increasing by addition) is said to take place where one or more of several beneficiaries dies before the testator and his share is added on to the share of others, i.e. it "accresces".

The first place to look for guidance on this matter is the will itself and hopefully it will make the position clear. If it does not, the following fairly simple presumptions will apply. These presumptions derive from the case of *Paxton's Trustees v Cowie* (1886) 13 R. 1191. It does not matter whether the property is heritable or moveable, nor is the nature of the bequest important, e.g. whether it is special, general or residuary, in liferent or in fee.

If the legacy is joint, e.g. ". . . to John and Jean", there will be accretion. Thus if John dies before the testator, the entire legacy goes to Jean, i.e. John's share accresces to Jean's.

If the legacy is several, e.g. ". . . to John and Jean equally between them" or ". . . to John and Jean share and share alike" (or similar words of severance), accretion does not apply. So if John dies before the testator, his share of the legacy would (probably) fall into the residue of the estate.

However, there is a pitfall for the unwary. If there is a legacy to a class of persons, e.g. "my nieces", even if there are words of severance, accretion would be presumed to apply. In *Roberts' Trustees v Roberts* (1903) 5 F. 541, a one-third share was left to each of three children. Dividing anything into three parts is a very clear example of severance. However, in context, accretion applied in respect of a predeceasing son's share, since it was a bequest to a class. A particular problem could arise where members of an apparent class are named individually; thus, ". . . to my sons John and James a one half share of . . . " may not be a class bequest, since they are named as individuals. Remember that all of these presumptions are subject to express provisions in the will.

A practical illustration may help, if we consider whether accretion would apply in the following circumstances, assuming that, in each case, party A dies before the testator.

(1) ". . . to A and B": this is a clear example of a joint legacy and A's share accresces to B.

(2) ". . . to A and B equally between them": because there are words of severance, accretion does not apply.

(3) ". . . to my nieces A and B": this is a joint legacy, so accretion would apply.

(4) ". . . to my nieces share and share alike": although there are words of severance, the bequest is to a class, so accretion would apply.

(5) ". . . to my nieces A and B equally between them": this is more problematic, since it is probably not a class gift, because the parties are individually named. Accretion would not apply, although the presumption would yield to the precise wording of the will.

Finally, accretion can take place as a result of events other than the death of a potential beneficiary. If, as happened in *Fraser's Trustees v Fraser*, 1980 S.L.T. 211, a legacy is provided for A and B with words of severance, but the provision in favour of B is revoked by the testator, there is no accretion and the original provision in favour of B falls into intestate succession. If there are no words of severance, however, the bequest would be joint and A would take the entire share by accretion.

10. EXECUTRY PRACTICE

10–01 Succession is an area that involves a great deal of legal theory and also a great many potential complications putting that theory into practice. The task of ensuring that a deceased's estate is correctly administered falls to the executor. This, therefore, is an office of no small responsibility and merits separate consideration, even if exhaustive coverage of the area is not possible in a book of this size.

APPOINTMENT OF THE EXECUTOR

10–02 Executors come in two main categories. If the deceased left a will, he should also have made arrangements in that will for the appointment of an executor, who has the resulting title of executor-nominate. However, if the estate is intestate, the court will have to appoint an executor, who is given the title of executor-dative.

A professionally drafted will should always nominate an executor. A trust disposition and settlement may appoint the same person(s) as executor(s) and as trustee(s). This is perfectly in order and, indeed, quite normal. Although the two functions do overlap, they are distinct in law. It is possible, however, especially with informal or home-made wills, that no executor is nominated. It is also possible that a nominated executor shall decline to act, become incapax (incapable of carrying out the duties) or even die before taking up office. The Executors (Scotland) Act 1900 s.3 provides that, in any of these eventualities, the testamentary trustees (if appointed and having capacity) will be deemed executors-nominate. Where there are no such trustees, or if there is a persisting problem such as lack of capacity, the office of executor falls on any general disponee, universal legatory or residuary legatee. In context, a general disponee is found where the estate contains heritable property, whilst a universal legatory is found where the estate is entirely moveable. A residuary legatee is anyone entitled to the residue of the estate. If there are several legatees, they are all required to accept or decline the office expressly.

If it is not possible to identify an executor-nominate, or if the estate is intestate, it is necessary therefore to appoint an executor-dative. To do this, an application must be lodged in the form of a petition to the sheriff court of the sheriffdom in which the deceased was domiciled.

The parties entitled to appointment are, in order of priority:

(1) the surviving spouse, if that spouse has prior rights which exhaust the estate;
(2) the deceased's next-of-kin (relations entitled to succeed under intestate succession);
(3) other persons in the order in which they are entitled to succeed according to the rules of intestate succession;

(4) creditors of the deceased;
(5) legatees;
(6) the procurator fiscal or a judicial factor.

At common law, "next-of-kin" referred to the class nearest in degree to the deceased with at least one surviving member. It would be perfectly in order for a surviving spouse, particularly if elderly, to decline the office and for, say, the eldest son to petition for appointment. In cases where there are two or more applicants within the same category, they are all entitled to be appointed jointly.

An executor-dative is often required to lodge a bond of caution (pronounced "kay-shun") with the sheriff. This is a guarantee that the executor will correctly perform the duties of the office and is usually provided by an insurance company to indemnify creditors and beneficiaries against losses caused by fraud or negligence. A bond of caution is not required where a spouse or civil partner inherits the entire estate through prior rights, nor is it required for "small" intestate estates (see below). The 2016 Act also provides for the making of further exceptions, though it was recently held that this does not allow the courts discretion to waive the requirement (*Garnett's Executor, Applicant*, 2017 S.L.T. (Sh. Ct) 50).

OVERVIEW OF THE EXECUTOR'S DUTIES

Regardless of exactly how an executor has assumed office, his main **10–03**
function is to ensure that the deceased's estate is correctly distributed and "wound up". In so doing, the executor must discharge a number of duties, which can be summarised as follows.

(1) To arrange for the safekeeping of the estate until such time as he can obtain "confirmation", i.e. the legal authority to administer the estate.
(2) To represent the deceased in legal matters.
(3) To frame an "inventory" of the deceased's estate and lodge this with the local commissary office. The inventory forms the basis of the executor's confirmation.
(4) To ingather the estate. Some items, such as bank accounts, are personal to the deceased and must be liquidated. Others, such as heritable property or stocks and shares, can be transferred to beneficiaries intact.
(5) To pay debts and liabilities, according to statutory rules.
(6) To distribute the estate to the beneficiaries, according either to the will or rules of intestacy.

A number of issues may arise during the discharge of the executor's duties. The most common of these will now be dealt with in turn.

SAFEKEEPING OF THE ESTATE

10–04 An executor cannot proceed to "intromit" with (administer) the estate until he has obtained confirmation from the sheriff. This is often misunderstood by the lay person. Thus, even although pressurised by members of the family to start distribution immediately after the funeral is over (if not sooner), the executor must firmly decline to do so. The confirmation is, in fact, the executor's legal title to intromit.

If an executor (or anyone else) intromits with the property of the deceased without having confirmation, this intromission is counted as being "vitious". A "vitious intromitter" may be held personally liable for any debts of the deceased that cannot ultimately be paid due to his vitious intromission (*Fraser v Gibb* (1784) Mor. 3921). This could be the case even when there was no actual fraudulent intention.

It should be noted that liability for vitious intromission is only to creditors. The executor is not generally liable to disappointed beneficiaries, although where the executor is a practicing solicitor, vitious intromission may constitute professional negligence (*Steven v Hewats* [2013] CSOH 61).

REPRESENTING THE DECEASED

10–05 In carrying out his duties, an executor acts as the legal representative of the deceased. He is debtor to the deceased's creditors and creditor to the deceased's debtors and is entitled to sue for the recovery of debts due to the deceased. He may have to perform or conclude contracts undertaken by the deceased, although not if they involve an element of *delectus personae* (choice of person), i.e. where the personal skill or qualities of the deceased were relied on. An obvious example is the deceased's contract of employment, which dies with him.

DRAFTING THE INVENTORY

10–06 This is a practical skill that cannot be obtained merely by reading books. Nevertheless, it is useful to make a few comments about this crucial part of the executry process. It stands to reason that every estate is different; the following are very general rules, which should only be applied after due care and enquiry.

The inventory has a two-fold purpose of, first, calculating whether any inheritance tax ("IHT") will be payable and, secondly, of obtaining the actual confirmation. Items in the inventory are recorded in a document called a "confirmation form C1" or "Form C1" for short. The executor must value each item in the estate. Valuation is not always an exact science, although care should be taken not to either significantly overvalue or undervalue the estate. The general rule is that all assets are valued at open market value as at the date of death.

If it appears that IHT will be payable (on which see Ch.2), additional documentation must also be completed. As mentioned previously, IHT is a very specialist area which is beyond the scope of this book.

The most commonly-encountered assets, with relevant commentary, are now considered in turn.

Heritable property

The way in which a heritable property is described for confirmation **10–07** depends on how the title has been registered. For a title presently recorded in the General Register of Sasines, the description must be sufficient to identify the subjects. If the title has been registered in the Land Register, a description is not necessarily required, but it is essential that the registered title number is quoted.

Although already discussed in previous chapters, there are three points worth re-iterating at this stage regarding the deceased's interest in heritable property. First, it is common for those who share use of heritable property to take title in joint names; only the value of the deceased's interest forms part of the estate. Secondly, in a related point, heritable property passing under a special destination does not form part of the deceased's estate for purposes of administration, although account must be taken of it for the calculation of IHT. Thirdly, the amount of any outstanding mortgage over heritable property must be deducted from its value.

Cash in house

Any balance of cash in the deceased's possession, no matter how small, should **10–08** be handed over to the executor and accounted for in the inventory.

Household furniture and personal effects

It is not usually necessary to list all the separate items of furnishing within the **10–09** deceased's house; one global sum is sufficient. It is a matter of judgement whether it is necessary to go to the expense of a professional valuation. If the estate is likely to be subject to IHT, a professional valuation is recommended, otherwise, a reasonable approximation will probably suffice. Items such as jewellery, antiques or specialist hobby equipment may also warrant professional valuation. A valuer will normally produce a detailed list of items; reference may be made to this report on the Form C1.

The valuation is what the effects are worth as at date of death, not what it might cost to replace them of new (as in an insurance policy). In the case of one of a married couple or civil partnership dying, the furniture and effects in the house would be confirmed to in respect of a half-share, unless the true facts were different.

Motor car

10–10 As explained in Ch.3, in professional practice a motor car is not normally counted as part of the household effects. A car may be valued by using one of the trade guides or obtaining a professional valuation. The car should be identified by its make, model and registration number. There are no presumptions about half-shares in cars.

Bank and building society accounts

10–11 These figures can be obtained from the institution itself with interest accrued to date of death. Having been informed of the death of its customer, the institution should freeze the account, unless it is a joint account. With joint accounts, the inventory should state the proportion contributed by the deceased. There is no presumption about half-shares.

Company shares

10–12 Valuation of shares in a publicly quoted Plc is straightforward and, in practice, is usually carried out by a stockbroker. The stockbroker should be informed that the valuation is for the purpose of confirmation. The shares are valued as at date of death.

Shares in a private company or in a Plc whose shares are not quoted on the stock market will require professional valuation. The basis of valuation is the price the shares would (in theory) fetch on the open market on the assumption that the prospective purchasers had available to them all the information which a prudent buyer might reasonably require. In practice, the transfer of shares in private companies is often restricted, but this is not taken into account for purposes of the valuation.

Moveable debts

10–13 Unlike the heritable debts, moveable debts are not directly deducted from the listed assets but are accounted for separately in another part of the inventory form. Thus, the global values of deceased estates, sometimes published in local newspapers, do not always reveal an entirely accurate picture. An estate might appear to be substantial but the moveable debts might, in fact, considerably reduce the real value.

OBTAINING CONFIRMATION

10–14 Once the inventory has been prepared (and any IHT paid) the executor can proceed to apply for confirmation. The executors are required to swear that, to the best of their knowledge and belief, the inventory contains a full and accurate account of the deceased's estate. If there is a will and any relevant codicils, the executors also have to swear that these are the only operative ones known to them. One executor may take the oath on behalf of all of the executors. It may be sworn before a justice of the peace, certain officials at the sheriff court or a notary public. Most solicitors are also notaries public.

The signed inventory must be lodged with the sheriff clerk of the commissariot in which the deceased was domiciled, accompanied by the will appointing the executor-nominate or, in the case of an executor-dative, a bond of caution (if required). The sheriff clerk will, in due course, issue the confirmation. When the sheriff issues confirmation, this is, to all intents and purposes, a copy of the inventory lodged by the executor but with an official warrant to the executor to intromit with the estate.

It is worth noting at this point that a simplified confirmation procedure can be accessed for "small" estates. At the time of writing, a "small" estate is one whose gross value, i.e. before deduction of debts, is not more than £36,000. This figure can be raised by statutory instrument, the most recent increase occurring in February 2012; the previous figure was £30,000. Under the small estates procedure, the sheriff clerk will give assistance in completing the inventory, and there is no requirement for a separate petition for the appointment of an executor-dative, should such appointment be required. No one is obliged to use this system, if they do not wish to. The sheriff clerk must be satisfied that there is no competition for appointment of the executor, that the executor is the person entitled to be appointed and that the value of the gross estate does not exceed £36,000. Once the inventory is completed, the subsequent procedure is identical and the sheriff clerk is unable to provide further advice on the administration of the estate.

INGATHERING THE ESTATE

Armed with this document, the executor now has title to collect and **10–15** ingather all the listed property, both heritable and moveable, which belonged to the deceased. The confirmation (or separate certificate of confirmation for any individual item on the inventory) can now be exhibited to whoever is in possession or custody, or whoever registers the item, such as a bank. The item will be encashed, sold, endorsed into the executor's name or transferred to a beneficiary. As money comes into the hands of the executor, he may proceed to pay off debts due by the deceased.

It is not uncommon for an executor to find that he has omitted, misdescribed or undervalued part of the estate, e.g. a previously undiscovered bank passbook that the deceased had hidden away and of which the executor had no knowledge. In such a case, if confirmation has already been granted, the executor will prepare a corrective inventory incorporating the additional item. The executor will be granted an "eik" (pronounced "eek") to his confirmation. An eik is simply an additional confirmation that supplements or corrects the original document. If the original executor has died and additional property is discovered, it is not competent for his successor to apply for an eik. Instead, the new executor would be able to apply for confirmation *ad omissa* (in respect of things omitted).

If all the executors in whose favour the confirmation was granted die or become incapacitated, creditors and other interested parties can apply for confirmation *ad non executa* (in respect of property not administered) and this authorises them to complete the administration of the estate.

If the deceased owned estate outwith Scotland, confirmation may not be acceptable in that country. Thus it may be necessary for the confirmation to be re-sealed in the probate register of that country. A Scottish confirmation is recognised throughout the UK by virtue of reciprocal arrangements (Administration of Estates Act 1971) and may include property in England, Wales or Northern Ireland, if the deceased had his domicile in Scotland.

PAYMENT OF DEBTS

10–16 As far as creditors are concerned, the executor is the same person as the deceased (*eadem persona cum defuncto*) and is liable to the creditors to the same extent as was the deceased. However, the liability of the executor is clearly limited to the amount of the deceased's estate. As observed in Ch.2, if the funds in the estate are not adequate to meet the claims of all creditors in full, then some debts will inevitably be written off; they are not transferred to the deceased's descendants.

Some debts are regarded as privileged, e.g. funeral expenses and certain fiscal debts. When privileged debts have been paid but the remaining estate is not enough to pay the ordinary creditors in full, all claims made within six months of the death rank pari passu (on an equal footing). The full order of payment of debts is set out below. Unless an executor is satisfied that the estate can meet all debts in full, he would be most unwise to pay any ordinary unsecured creditor until six months have expired from the date of death.

Even after the six month period has expired, the executor is still bound to pay any valid claim from a creditor, assuming he still has funds in hand to do so. If the executor is aware that valid debts have not been paid and he still distributes the whole estate to beneficiaries, he can find himself personally liable to pay such debts.

The executor must pay debts according to a statutory order, currently outlined by the Bankruptcy (Scotland) Act 2016. Debts are basically payable in the following order; each class must be paid in full before progressing to the next class. Claimants in each class rank pari passu.

(1) Deathbed and funeral expenses are payable before all others, even secured debts. Also included here are the expenses of confirmation and the executry administration.

(2) Secured debts speak for themselves. A secured creditor is in a good position in that he can generally enforce his debt at any time. If the secured property is worth more than the debt (including interest), the creditor must account for the surplus to the estate. If the security is worth less than the debt, the creditor can rank for the deficit

against the estate, but only as an ordinary creditor in respect of that proportion.

(3) Preferred debts, which in practice most commonly means wages owed to employees (up to certain statutory limits).

(4) Ordinary unsecured debts also speak for themselves. The vast majority of debts are unsecured.

(5) Inheritance tax, in practice, is paid first, often by means of a temporary overdraft, since confirmation cannot be obtained until it is paid. Nevertheless, it actually ranks last in order of priority. The point is academic; it stands to reason that if there is no estate, no IHT is payable.

If an executor believes that there is insufficient funds to cover the debts of the deceased, he should be advised, at an early date, to have a judicial factor or a trustee in bankruptcy appointed. If such an appointment takes place, the expenses of sequestration take precedence even over privileged debts. If an executor knows, or clearly ought to know, that an estate is insolvent and he fails to take appropriate steps, the executor's intromissions may count as vitious. In such a situation, the executor may be personally liable for the debts of the deceased.

Incidence of debts

Another matter to be addressed is what is called the "incidence" of debts. **10–17**
It has been observed several times that the distinction between heritable and moveable estate is still crucial in the law of succession. The question is bound to arise as to which parts of the estate are liable for which debts. The basic rule is simple: heritable debts are paid out of heritage and moveable debts out of the moveable estate. A debt is heritable if it is secured over heritable property. In a solvent estate, the incidence of debts is bound to affect prior rights (if the estate is intestate) and legal rights.

It has already been noted that problems can, and do, frequently arise when a heritable debt exists but the amount of the debt is covered by an insurance policy. Many mortgages have the capital sum covered by life assurance. Borrowers are often under the impression that, should they die during the life of the mortgage, the capital sum will automatically be repaid. It is necessary to underline the fact that a mortgage is a heritable debt and the proceeds of an insurance policy count as a moveable asset. The two do not automatically cancel one another out. A surviving spouse or civil partner, under intestate succession, may have a claim to the matrimonial home, but takes it subject to any existing security. Since the proceeds of the policy are moveable, these may be subject to claims for legal rights.

If the will is well drafted, it may specify its own incidence of debts. So, if a house is left to a beneficiary "free of debt", then any outstanding mortgage has to be paid off out of the residue of the estate.

DISTRIBUTION

10–18 Ensuring that the estate is correctly distributed among the deceased's beneficiaries is, of course, one of the primary functions of the executor. This will be done either according to the rules of testacy or intestacy as appropriate. Potential claimants of legal rights should be notified and asked to elect whether or not to claim. Reasonable time must be given to ensure that all who might wish to claim have had the chance to do so. The executor is not required to wait indefinitely, however, and normal practice is that if the estate is solvent, funds will begin being paid out after around 12 months. Beneficiaries under wills frequently complain that they have to wait too long for their money, though, in fact, this is often due more to perception than to reality.

DISCHARGE OF EXECUTORS

10–19 The vast majority of executries end with the successful winding up of the deceased's estate. In their own interests, executors should normally seek formal discharge at the close of their administration. Alongside various other related matters, discharge is considered further in the next chapter.

11. TRUSTS

Trusts, in one form or another, have been with us for centuries and remain an important part of private law. They can just as easily arise inter vivos as mortis causa, but only the latter will be considered in any detail here. Since executors are trustees by statutory definition, there is considerable overlap between the law of trusts and of succession. Nevertheless, there are distinctions. The executor obtains confirmation, ingathers the estate, pays the debts and then distributes property to beneficiaries. At that point, the executor's duties are at an end. If there are continuing trust purposes, the administration of these begins when property or funds are transferred to the trustees. Even if (as is common) the executors and trustees are the same individuals, the two roles are separate. **11–01**

NATURE AND LEGAL BASIS

At its simplest, a trust is a legal arrangement whereby one party (the "truster") transfers property to another (the "trustee") for the benefit of a third (the "beneficiary"). It is possible for more than one person to occupy any of these roles, and indeed it is particularly common to appoint more than one trustee, and/or identify more than one beneficiary. **11–02**

As its name suggests, this arrangement is based first and foremost on trust. One party entrusts property and duties to another and, in so doing, relies on his honesty, fair play and obedience to instructions. In former times, trusts were largely governed by common law, but there were considerable statutory inroads made in the 19th and 20th centuries. The main governing statutes now are the Trusts (Scotland) Acts of 1921 ("the 1921 Act") and 1961 ("the 1961 Act"). The common law does, however, still have an important role.

PRIVATE AND PUBLIC TRUSTS

Every trust will be either private or public. In a private trust, the beneficiaries will always be private individuals, either expressly named or easily identified as a private class, e.g. "my nephews". Only beneficiaries or others with a direct interest have any title to sue. If a private mortis causa trust fails before it even comes into effect, the property will revert to the deceased's estate. In practice, the majority of trusts are private. **11–03**

A public trust, as the name would suggest, is for the benefit of the public, or a proportion or class of the public. Normally, such a trust will be of an educational, religious or charitable nature. The Charities and Trustee Investment (Scotland) Act 2005 ("the 2005 Act") introduced major changes to the law affecting charities in Scotland, setting up the Office of the Scottish Charity Regulator ("OSCR"). There is now a public register of charities and the OSCR has wide powers to monitor, investigate and take action to ensure good practice and protect assets where appropriate. Section 7 of the 2005 Act also provides statutory definitions of what are recognised as charitable purposes. In the case of a public trust, any member of the public having an interest to do so has a title to sue.

Occasionally, there has been doubt as to whether a particular trust is public or private. In *Salvesen's Trustees v Wye*, 1954 S.C. 440, there was a legacy to "poor relatives, friends or acquaintances". The court held that the beneficiaries' connection with the testator was the dominant factor rather than their poverty and, accordingly, it was a private trust. On the other hand, in the older case of *Andrews v Ewart's Trustees* (1886) 13 R. (HL) 69, a trust set up for the establishment of a school was held to be a public trust and title to sue rested with members of the public who might wish to avail themselves of this educational provision.

CONSTITUTION

11–04 Ideally, a trust should be constituted expressly, although no technical wording is required. A trust can be constituted by implication provided there is a clear intention to do so. If the trust is testamentary, writing is an absolute requirement, as in the case of any bequest.

There are two main requirements for a valid trust. There must be actual property, heritable or moveable, and there must be some purpose for this property being held by trustees. The purpose may, in practice, be very simple, such as holding property until a beneficiary attains a particular age.

A mortis causa trust can only be created by a testamentary writing, normally a trust disposition and settlement. Such a trust does not come into effect until the death of the truster. As long as the truster is living and competent, he can revoke the testamentary writing. If the purposes of a mortis causa trust fail or do not exhaust the estate, the surplus property can be claimed by those entitled by succession, e.g. a residuary legatee or heirs in intestacy.

TRUSTEES

11–05 At the heart of the common law of trusts is the concept of property vesting in trustees. A trustee has legal title to the property and effectively owns it, but his title is not beneficial to himself. The beneficiaries, whether of property, capital or income have the beneficial interest or *jus crediti* (right to the benefit). Therefore, a trustee is the legal owner of the property but only in order to administer it on behalf of the beneficiaries.

Although s.2 of the 1921 Act identifies a number of parties expressly deemed to be trustees, the common law also applies to any person in a position of trust generally, such as a company director, a partner on behalf of his firm or an agent on behalf of his principal. The 2005 Act introduced a new form of trustee, the charity trustee, who now has clear statutory duties and for whom mismanagement can also be interpreted as misconduct.

No specific form of consent to acting as a trustee is insisted upon by law, but writing is clearly desirable, especially in the case of someone being appointed (assumed) to an existing trust. A trustee normally carries out his duties gratuitously, although the responsibilities are onerous and the courts tend to be fairly strict in the area of enforcement.

DUTIES OF TRUSTEES

The actual duties of trustees are largely governed by common law although, **11–06**
as stated above, certain trustees are governed by statutory provisions. It is obvious that a trustee must administer the trust estate in line with the directions of the truster. In many ways, the common law duties of a trustee are similar (though not identical) to that of an executor. The main duties of a trustee can be summarised as follows.

(1) A trustee must ingather, administer and distribute the estate. Frequently, in a mortis causa trust, the trustees and executors are the same individuals.

(2) Trustees are under a general duty to complete title to property which forms part of the trust estate. This is strictly imposed.

(3) A trustee is expected to exercise due care. The standard of care is that of a reasonably prudent person in the management of his own affairs (*Rae v Meek* (1889) 16 R. (HL) 31).

(4) The office of trustee is essentially one of *delectus personae* (choice of person) and demands his personal attention. He cannot delegate his ultimate responsibility to another party, although the 2005 Act allows trustees to select nominees and also to delegate investment and management of funds where the trust deed is silent.

(5) A trustee must not act in his own interests. This is also imposed strictly, so that a trustee's interests as an individual must not, even potentially, be brought into conflict with his duties as a trustee (*Aberdeen Railway Co v Blaikie Bros* (1853) 1 Macq. 461).

(6) The office of trustee is gratuitous and no trustee has the right to be paid unless there is express power to do so in the trust deed. Payment includes commission.

(7) Trustees must keep proper and adequate records of their intromissions both with capital and income. A beneficiary has the right to see any such documentation.

(8) Trustees must keep trust funds properly invested. The trust deed itself will frequently give wide powers to trustees or give fairly specific directions. At common law and in the absence of directions, trustees are restricted in their discretion, but under the 2005 Act (Pt 3) trustees generally have the same powers of investment as if they were beneficial owners. Their overarching duty in investment is to secure the best possible return to the trust.

POWERS OF TRUSTEES

11–07 When seeking to establish the powers of a trustee, the first place to look is the trust deed. Where the deed is silent, the trustees have powers implied by both common law and statute. The Court of Session may also exercise its *nobile officium* to give further powers to the trustees where the trust is unworkable.

The most basic common law power of trustees is to administer the trust on a day to day basis. The 1921 and 1961 Acts set out certain powers, provided they are not at variance with the provisions of the trust deed. These include the power to sell the estate, to grant leases, borrow money on the security of the estate, appoint agents and solicitors and grant all necessary deeds.

Where there is more than one trustee, all must be given the opportunity to attend meetings and to participate in the administration of the trust. Sometimes, the deed of trust may provide for a quorum, i.e. the number of trustees who must agree to the exercising of powers. In the absence of such a provision, the 1921 Act s.3(c) provides that a majority of accepting and surviving trustees is a valid quorum.

LIABILITY OF TRUSTEES

11–08 Trustees are not liable for the truster's debts beyond the value of the estate at their disposal. If trustees or executors discover that the inherited debts exceed the value of the estate, in their own interests they should take steps to have the estate sequestrated. If they do not, their own intromissions may count as vitious, leaving them with personal liability for the debts of the deceased.

Trustees are personally liable, jointly and severally, for any debts they incur in the course of their administration. However, they are entitled to reimbursement in full from the trust estate, provided the debts have been properly incurred. In most cases, this personal liability does not cause problems. The result may be otherwise if the assets of the trust estate were insufficient to cover the debts (*Muir v City of Glasgow Bank* (1879) 6 R. (HL) 21).

A trustee who is in breach of trust may well have to pay back all the loss this breach has caused to the trust estate. "Breach" can cover a wide variety of omissions and commissions, from fraud to negligence and in varying degrees. It would be breach of trust to fail to make proper provisions for investment of funds or to delay unreasonably in paying beneficiaries. More directly, it is a trustee's nightmare to make a mistake by, say, paying the wrong beneficiary or overpaying the correct one. A trustee may be personally liable for such errors, regardless of how they have arisen (*Morgan Guaranty Trust Co of New York v Lothian RC*, 1995 S.L.T. 299), although statutory protections do exist. Under s.32 of the 1921 Act, the court may grant relief to a trustee who has acted "honestly and reasonably".

Under s.29A of the 1921 Act (inserted by the 2016 Act), a trustee is not liable for incorrect distributions made due to an error of fact regarding the existence or non-existence of a person or relationship relevant to the purposes of the trust.

It is not unusual for a trust deed to include an indemnity clause stating that the trustees are not to be held personally liable for omissions, error or neglect. The courts have tended to interpret such clauses restrictively and have not allowed them to protect a trustee who is blatantly in breach of duty (*Knox v Mackinnon* (1888) 15 R. (HL) 83).

ASSUMPTION, RESIGNATION AND REMOVAL OF TRUSTEES

Unless the trust deed provides to the contrary, new trustees can be appointed **11–09** or assumed by existing trustees. From a practical point of view, such assumptions would normally be in writing and the 1921 Act provides appropriate styles. If there are two existing trustees, both must sign the deed of assumption. If there are more than two, a quorum is sufficient but, in practice, the signature of all trustees is desirable.

At common law a trustee had no power to resign but, under the 1921 Act, is entitled to do so unless he is a sole trustee or has accepted the office on condition of a legacy. An executor-dative has no power to resign. For his own protection, a resigning trustee should execute a formal minute of resignation to avoid any possible personal liability for the future acts of his co-trustees.

The court will normally, as a matter of course, remove a trustee on the grounds of mental incapacity, disability, absence or disappearance. The court also has the general power to remove a trustee on such grounds as gross negligence, wilful breach of trust or fraud, though this is a power which, historically, has been used only sparingly.

JUDICIAL FACTORS

A judicial factor is really a special kind of trustee, appointed by the court **11–10** to look after an estate where some element of protection is required or a degree of fair play has to be ensured. Examples relevant to this area of law would be where trustees are in deadlock or where all original or assumed trustees have died. A petition must be made stating the grounds, the name of the person to be appointed and the property to be taken into his charge. The person whose funds are in his care is called the "ward".

The judicial factor's authority to intromit with the estate is the extract decree of appointment, which has a similar effect to an executor's confirmation. Normally a judicial factor has all the general powers of a trustee, although, as shown in Ch.7, he is unable to exercise dispositive discretion.

TERMINATION OF TRUSTS

11–11 There are trusts that have existed in Scotland for generations, but most trusts come to an end sooner or later. An inter vivos trust can only be revoked subject to conditions, but in a mortis causa trust the testator can validly revoke the provisions at any time up to his death.

Trustees can normally only terminate a trust by administering the trust according to its stated purposes and making a final and total distribution (denuding) in favour of the beneficiaries. If the trust assets were distributed to the wrong beneficiaries, the trust would not be at an end even though the trustees had denuded.

Beneficiaries have very limited powers to request termination of a trust. Potentially, it is possible, provided they all consent and it does not prejudice the trustees in their proper administration or interfere with any alimentary rights.

DISCHARGE OF TRUSTEES

11–12 It is common sense for trustees to ask for a discharge before a final distribution is made to beneficiaries so as to avoid any future personal liability. Normally trustees will not denude until a discharge has been granted but, once it has been granted, they are bound to do so. To put it another way, a trust is not really at an end until the trustees are discharged.

The discharge can only cover what is within the knowledge of the party granting it. If a beneficiary grants a discharge unaware that a trustee has carried out a major fraud, he could still bring a challenge at a later date when the facts come to light. If, however, a beneficiary was aware that a breach of trust had taken place yet signed a discharge he would be personally barred from founding on the breach at a later date.

The strict legal effect of granting a discharge is to protect trustees from future liability under the trust and to close off any challenge to their intromissions. This does not mean that trustees who have been discharged are beyond all possible challenge. The correct approach would be for the aggrieved party to raise an action of reduction in respect of the discharge, e.g. that it was granted as a result of fraud, essential error or breach of trust. Such actions in respect of trustees are, fortunately, rare in practice.

APPENDIX 1: SAMPLE EXAMINATION QUESTIONS AND ANSWER PLANS

It was mentioned in the Preface that one of the intended purposes of this book is as a revision aid. It is appropriate, therefore, to provide some material that might assist those readers who are working towards an examination on the subject.

It is, of course, true that everyone is different, and that everyone has their own strategies whilst revising and preparing for examinations. However, there are a number of "tried and tested" approaches, and some basic comments regarding these may be helpful.

Similarly, it is neither hinted nor suggested that the outline answers presented here are some model of perfection, though they do represent what would commonly be accepted as a "good" to "very good" response. Everyone has his or her own form of expression, so the most important lesson is to ensure that as many salient points as possible are included in each answer.

GENERAL COMMENTS

(1) First and foremost, always remember that examinations are your opportunity to demonstrate your knowledge and understanding of the subject. Often, this is the only opportunity you will be given to do so. If you do not demonstrate sufficient knowledge and understanding, you will not pass the exam. Conversely, the more (accurate) knowledge and understanding you demonstrate, the higher the mark you will achieve. Every examination answer you present should reflect what you have learned; anything less is simply not doing yourself justice.

(2) Leading on from the above, there are three elements you should try to include in every examination answer to ensure you are giving a complete response. The first is to answer the question actually asked; it is surprising how many candidates forget to do this. The second is to give as full an explanation as you can for your answer; this allows you to demonstrate, and receive credit for, your knowledge. The third is to cite authority for your answer; this means providing the legal basis on which you have founded your conclusions.

(3) When actually answering the question, there is nothing wrong with considering the situation from all sides. Many legal problems lend themselves to seeing both sides (which is an important part of legal training), and every experienced lawyer knows that interpretation is often key. Having said that, the strongest answers tend to be those which do confidently provide a conclusion; do not to leave your response so open-ended that you appear to be inviting the examiner to choose the correct answer for you.

(4) When explaining your answer, there is a delicate balance to be struck

between demonstrating the extent of your knowledge and demonstrating your understanding of what is relevant to the specific question being asked. Do not simply regurgitate everything you have learned about the subject; instead, be selective and ensure that you are focusing on what is most pertinent.

(5) The importance of citing authority cannot be overstated. Lawyers, and examiners, look for statutes and reported cases to provide a sound foundation for legal arguments. Avoid like the plague the expression "I think"; whilst your opinion is obviously relevant, the important factor is why and how have you formed it. Make sure you can justify and illustrate your answer with legal authority, i.e. show what you have deduced or concluded from considering cases and statutes. You should identify the relevant authority, and explain how it supports your answer. When referring to statutes, ideally you should give the short title (including the year) and section number. When using a case, you should strive to provide the party names and year; if you can give the full citation, all the better, though this is not usually expected. Give a brief summary of the facts, and apply the *ratio decidendi* behind the decision. If you remember the facts and decision of a relevant case, but cannot remember the name, do still use it. It is far better to say "in a settled case" or "in *A v B*" rather than miss it out. On the other hand, do not simply "name drop" cases with no explanation; knowing a full citation is not impressive if you know nothing of the case itself.

(6) More generally, it is wise to go into an examination knowing exactly what you are expected to do and exactly how much time you will have in which to do it. This allows you to use your time strategically. Note carefully the number of marks given for each part of a question; this should give guidance as to how long you can afford to take. If you write a very long answer for a 2 mark question, you are potentially wasting your resources. If your paper is broken down into sections, a good tip is to allocate an appropriate amount of time to each section and rigidly stick to this, even if it means leaving an answer unfinished; you can always come back to it if you find you have enough time at the end.

(7) When you begin actually composing your responses, there is no harm in making rough notes and drafts. In fact, it can be very useful to sketch out a brief plan, including all the relevant legal points and authorities you can remember, before starting your "proper" answer. Draw a line through this rough work once you have finished; there is a universal concordat among examiners that they ignore anything indicated in this way; they have better things to do than to read your notes (and possible mistakes) as well as your main text.

(8) Finally, in terms of presenting your work, remember that examiners face an onerous task. They have to read and assess many scripts in a short period of time, whilst attempting to remain scrupulously fair. The process will run more smoothly if your responses are both tidy and easy to follow. At the very least, make sure your handwriting is legible; you might lose out on precious marks if the examiner simply cannot read what you have written, and this is little short of disastrous. Having said that, examiners do

appreciate that candidates are working under time pressures and so they do not expect excessively neat scripts. In keeping with the comments on rough work, if you make a mistake in your answer, simply put a line through it; you do not have the luxury of time required for the use of correction fluid!

SAMPLE QUESTIONS WITH ANSWERS

Question 1

(a) Give a detailed explanation of a survivor's housing right under the prior rights applicable on intestacy.

(b) If the deceased owned two homes, what effect does this have on the financial provision available to the widow under prior rights?

(c) Castor is the second of two children of the third of four brothers of his Aunt Matilda. Matilda is survived by three sisters and all her brothers apart from the third, who died some years ago. She is also survived by her elderly widowed mother. The total net value of her estate is £56,000, of which £50,000 is heritable and £6,000 is moveable. Giving reasons for your answer, explain how much Castor will be due from Matilda's estate.

(a) Housing right in intestacy

This is a straightforward question on substantive law. The key to answering it is simply to ensure that you include all relevant information, including citation of authority, and present it in a logical order to the examiner. Take care to ensure you confine your answer to what is being asked; it might be tempting to explain other prior rights here as well, but doing so will not accrue any marks, since only the *housing right* has been asked for.

So, you should identify that under s.8 of the Succession (Scotland) Act 1964, a surviving spouse (or civil partner) is entitled to the ownership or tenancy of any one house owned or tenanted by the deceased at the time of death. You should explain that the *survivor* must have been ordinarily resident in the house in question at the time of the deceased's death. It is not a requirement that the deceased was ordinarily resident.

Also state the maximum value of this benefit, currently £473,000. (You should check this figure as part of your revision.) If the interest of the deceased exceeds that figure, the survivor is entitled to a sum of £473,000 only. The property is taken subject to any existing secured loan, the outstanding amount of which is deducted from the value. Frequently, the deceased may only have owned a one half *pro indiviso* share in the property, due to its being held in joint names. In that case, the survivor takes the deceased's half share, up to a value of £473,000. If the title was taken subject to a special destination, the half share passes automatically to the survivor; in such a case, it would be unnecessary to use the dwelling house right to claim the property.

You should also explain that if the house forms part of subjects included with a tenancy, or where it forms part of subjects used by the deceased for the purposes of a trade, profession or occupation, a cash sum would normally be paid instead of claiming the house itself. If the deceased owned more than one house *and* the survivor was ordinarily resident in both of them at the time of death, the survivor may take only one and has a period of six months to elect which one to take.

(b) Financial provision

This is another substantive law question, so the approach is exactly the same. However, again you must take care; it may not immediately be apparent what this question is asking, so make sure you read it carefully and answer accordingly.

Identify that under s.9 of the Succession (Scotland) Act 1964, where a deceased is intestate the surviving spouse or civil partner is entitled to claim a financial provision of £89,000, or £50,000 if there are surviving children or representatives of the deceased. (Again, you should have checked that these figures are up to date.) Also explain that if there is both heritable and moveable property in the estate after satisfaction of any other relevant prior rights, the financial provision is paid proportionately out of both heritable and moveable estate.

Finally, apply this to the question actually asked, by explaining that this would be the case here, since there is a second house and only one can be claimed under the dwellinghouse right.

(c) Aunt Matilda

This is a problem-solving question, whereby you must apply your knowledge and understanding to a "real life" situation. This sort of question may fluster candidates in the heat of the moment, since the wording may be initially difficult to follow. Read it carefully and take your time to make sense of the family situation being outlined; it might help to draw a "family tree". You can always draw your pen through it after you have attempted the question.

You should identify that since Matilda died intestate, without spouse or children, her entire estate counts as free estate (or dead's part). The free estate is claimed by the highest ranking claimant (or claimants if more than one rank equally with each other) as determined by s.2 of the Succession (Scotland) Act 1964. Since there are no children (who rank first), the free estate will be claimed by the surviving parent and siblings of the deceased. According to the rules of division, the free estate would first be divided into two half-shares, one going to the mother and the other being divided among the siblings; in the latter case, representation applies.

The fact that the estate is a mixture of heritable and moveable property is no more than a distraction since the division of free estate does not differentiate between the two. Accordingly, £28,000 would be claimed by Matilda's mother, and £28,000 would be available for distribution among the siblings. Since one sibling has pre-deceased (i.e. Castor's father) leaving two children to represent (one of which is Castor himself), not all the claimants are in the same degree of relationship to the deceased. Therefore, the division will be *per stirpes*. Those who are nearest to the deceased, her brothers and sisters, would each receive £4,000. The £4,000 that would have been claimed by Castor's father is claimable by Castor and his own sibling and would be divided equally; therefore, Castor's share is £2,000.

Question 2

(a) In which circumstances may conditions attached to a legacy be set aside and the legacy paid notwithstanding?

(b) What are the effects on other claimants of a child discharging any claim to legitim (i) before and (ii) after the death of his parent?

(c) Gregory dies leaving net estate of £195,000. In his will he directs that his house (value £150,000) is to be sold and the proceeds shared between Gladys, a young lady with whom he has been having a passionate affair, and the benevolent fund of his former army regiment. His moveable estate is valued at £45,000 and is left in entirety to Gladys. Gregory separated from his wife Clarinda 10 years ago, but there was no divorce or judicial separation. Their twin sons, Bill and Ben, live with Gregory, as does Gregory's widowed mother who has kept house since Clarinda moved out. Clarinda, Bill, Ben and Gregory's mother are all very angry and affronted at Gregory's will and are determined to press for every last penny to which they are entitled. Assuming that Gregory was sane when he made his will and that it was validly executed, how much, if anything, might each claimant get? Give an explanation to justify your conclusions.

(a) Setting aside conditions in a will

This is another substantive law question, but it is actually very open-ended; you would have to gauge carefully how many marks are assigned to it so as to ensure that you do not get carried away and write far more than the question is worth. Some areas worth including would be:

(1) *Void conditions*, where a condition is set aside on the grounds that it is uncertain, illegal, immoral or contrary to public policy. If the condition is set aside, the legacy can be paid without "strings attached". If, however, there is no obvious beneficiary, the entire legacy provision will fail. Whether the condition ought to be set aside is judged on a case-by-case basis. So, in *Fraser v Rose* (1849), a condition forbidding the legatee from living with her mother was set aside, whilst in *Balfour's Trustees v Johnston* (1936), a condition forbidding the legatee from associating with a certain orphan was not. In *McCaig v University of Glasgow* (1907), instructions to use the estate for the erection of towers and statues in the testator's honour was struck down as being of no benefit to anyone.

(2) *Repugnancy*, where conditions attached to a legacy are inconsistent with the main tenor of the legacy itself. One example would be where a legacy is given in full fee but trustees are then directed to hold the capital and pay only the revenue to the beneficiary. The direction to the trustees

would be repugnant and the beneficiary would receive the full fee. In *Dow v Kilgour's Trustees* (1877), a testator directed that an annuity be purchased for the legatee, but this was repugnant since the legatee could immediately have sold the annuity; the legatee was instead entitled to payment of the lump sum which would have been used to buy the annuity.

(3) *Accumulation of income*, as a rule of thumb, is not permitted for more than 21 years after the death of a testator. The legal development of this area began with the case of *Thelluson v Woodford* (1799), where a testator validly directed that his estate should be invested and the income paid out only after two generations of his descendants had died. Criticism of the decision led to the Accumulations Act 1800, with the current law largely now contained in the Trusts (Scotland) Act 1961. Under the statutory provisions it is perfectly legitimate to accumulate for up to 21 years but, after this period has elapsed, the surplus income must be distributed to those who would have been entitled if accumulation had not been directed in the first place.

(4) *Liferents* cannot be created in favour of parties not yet born. The Law Reform (Miscellaneous Provisions) (Scotland) Act 1968 provides that it is not possible to create a liferent in favour of someone who is not alive or *in utero* at the date of the creator's death. If a testator attempts to do so, the liferent property will belong absolutely to the beneficiary at the date when he becomes entitled to the liferent, provided he is aged 18; if he is under that age, he must wait until attaining the age of 18.

(b) Discharge of legitim

A good, classic question, although few people actually do want to discharge legal rights before the death of a parent. The first point to make is crucial: the legitim fund is fixed as at date of death and (leaving aside payment of interest on the principal sum) does not increase or decrease in value. The actual value of the fund is not affected by discharge of legitim before or after the parent's death. However, the potential difference in the effect on other claimants, i.e. siblings or their representatives, is substantial.

(i) Discharge before death

If a child renounces his legal rights before the death of his parent he is deemed (for this purpose only) to have died before his parent and to have left no issue to represent (even if the true situation is different). The result is that the amount available to other claimants is bound to be more. If there are three children, for example, and one has predeceased leaving no issue, the legitim fund will be divided in two rather than in three. Any renunciation of legal rights before the death of a parent would have to be express; it could not be implied.

(ii) Discharge after death

If the renunciation takes place after the death of the parent, the effect is different. Because legal rights are fixed at the moment of the parent's death, nothing that takes place after that death can change the amounts designated for each claimant. Thus the portion of the legitim fund which has been renounced falls into dead's part or residue, as the case may be. So, if there are three children, one of whom renounces legal rights after the death of his parent, his two siblings can still only claim one third of the legitim fund each, the remaining third going to dead's part or residue. A discharge of legal rights after the death of the parent could be express or it could be implied since the acceptance of a legacy provision, whether of heritable or moveable estate, is deemed to be in full and final settlement of legal rights unless (unlikely) the will expressly states otherwise.

(c) Gregory's will

This is another good example of a problem question. As before, make sure you understand everything correctly before tackling the relevant legal issues.

Starting with the heritable property, there is no member of the family who can prevent Gregory disposing of it. A widow's dwellinghouse right only applies in intestacy and she must have been ordinarily resident in the house in question. Clarinda fails on both counts. The fact that Gregory directs his house to be sold does not alter the fact that the property was heritable at the time of his death. It will therefore be sold and the proceeds divided as instructed.

However, legal rights *are* applicable here, since they can be claimed regardless of whether there is a will or not. Clarinda can therefore claim *jus relictae*, and the children can claim legitim, out of the moveable estate. Thus Clarinda can claim £15,000 (one third of the net moveable estate) and the children share the legitim fund of £15,000 (also one third of the net moveable estate) between them; division is per capita, since both are in the same degree of relationship to the deceased. The remaining moveable estate (the residue) will be distributed according to the will.

Unfortunately for Gregory's mother, she has no claim; a parent cannot claim legal rights, and a parent's claim on any free estate is only applicable on intestacy.

Assuming that the house is sold for its exact valuation figure, the final distribution would therefore be as follows:

GLADYS	
Half share of house	£75,000
Residue	£15,000
BENEVOLENT FUND	
Half share of house	£75,000
CLARINDA	
Jus relictae	£15,000

BILL	
Share of legitim	£7,500
BEN	
Share of legitim	£7,500
MOTHER	Nil
	£195,000

Question 3
(a) Mr Grimm is a widower in his seventies. Although not rich, Mr Grimm is quite comfortable, owning his house outright, a car, a considerable portfolio of shares and some interesting paintings. In addition, he has some items of jewellery which belonged to his late wife and which are expected to appreciate considerably in the near future. Grimm's only relatives are his two sons, one of whom is very close to him, but the other is the "black sheep" of the family. Grimm wants to make a testamentary provision which will favour the one son and exclude the other, at least as far as this is possible.

(b) The late John, a bachelor, was the middle of five children, with two older sisters and two younger brothers. Only John's youngest brother, George, married. George had two children but died before John. The other brother and the two sisters survived John; their parents both died many years ago. George's widow alleges that John signed a will leaving his estate to be shared equally among his brothers and sisters and thus, she claims, she is entitled to a share. Explain the effect on the division of John's estate if he had (i) left such a will and (ii) died intestate.

(a) Mr Grimm and exclusion of the "black sheep"

You should explain that if Mr Grimm dies testate, the only claim which either of his sons could make against his estate is that of legal rights. Children can claim against a notional legitim fund which is either a one half-share of the net moveable estate where there is no surviving spouse (as in this case) or a one third-share where there is a surviving spouse. Thus, even if Grimm tries to exclude his wayward son from the succession, he cannot do so as the son can claim (in this case) one quarter of the net moveable estate in spite of anything the will says. All Grimm can actually do is to minimise the extent of his moveable estate. He could give a substantial amount to his favourite son here and now, which would not require to be collated later since, presumably, the favoured son would not claim legitim. Another possibility is the conversion of as much of his moveable property as possible into actual heritage.

(b) John and the family problem

Not all the facts are known here, and this is acknowledged by the question inviting consideration of two possibilities. It is worth pointing out briefly that where it is known that a person made a will but, at the time of his death, it cannot be found, the presumption is that the deceased destroyed that will *animo revocandi*.

(i) John did leave such a will

The first matter to dispose of is George's widow's claim. Unless the will expressly provided for her, she could not take any share in place of George, since George had died before his brother and it is a basic rule of succession that a legatee must survive the deceased in order to acquire a vested right. For the same reason, George's children similarly have no claim; representation only applies on intestacy, and the only practical exception to the survivorship rule in testacy (previously known as the *conditio si institutus sine liberis decesserit*, now statutory under s.6 of the Succession (Scotland) Act 2016) would not apply here since the institute of the legacy (George) was not a direct descendant of the testator (John).

The broader matter, then, is what will actually happen to George's notional share. Does it automatically accresce to the siblings, does it fall into the residue, or does it fall into intestacy? It is worth underlining that the first place to look is the actual will in the hope that precise instructions are set out there. If they are not, the basic presumptions apply but even these will differ according to the wording of the will. If a legacy is joint, "to X and Y", there will be accretion. So, if X dies before the testator, his share accresces to that of Y. However, if there are words of severance, such as "share and share alike", there is a presumption against accretion, unless the legacy is to a class of persons, such as "my brothers and sisters". There is further complication that if the members of the class are specifically named, there is a presumption against accretion. It would be difficult to give a firm conclusion to this question, so there is nothing wrong here with considering various possibilities.

(ii) John having died intestate

If John was intestate, his entire estate would have to be dealt with as dead's part, since there is no surviving spouse and no children. The estate will be shared out among the class making up his brothers and sisters. Whilst there is representation in respect of the dead's part, that representation is only in favour of descendants and not to a spouse of the predeceasing claimant. Thus, since George left children, they could represent their father and claim his share *per stirpes*. If there were no direct descendants of George, the estate would be divided per capita among the surviving brother and the two sisters. In either case, George's widow would have no claim.

Question 4

(a) Kate has died, and her will leaves her nephew, Cuthbert, the heritable property known as Claybogs Farm. It has always been Cuthbert's wish and expectation to own and farm that property and his aunt had acquainted him with the contents of her will some time ago. Very shortly before her death, Kate sold the farm for £400,000. The proceeds of the sale are still in the hands of her solicitor. Cuthbert is disappointed that the farm has been sold but is looking forward to receiving £400,000 instead. Advise Cuthbert.

(b) Augustus has no relatives, so he leaves his house and a portfolio of shares worth £50,000 to Bill (a friend) whom failing to Freda (another friend). Bill, a bachelor, enjoys ownership of the house and shares for a few months but then dies unexpectedly. Freda is wondering if the house and shares will now come to her. Advise Freda.

(a) Cuthbert and Claybogs

It looks as though Cuthbert's great expectations are about to be dashed. It may well be that Aunt Kate had intended to leave him the money instead of the farm. Unfortunately, she did not change her will and, where a will is perfectly clear and unambiguous, the courts will uphold it. The legacy of the farm is specific, because the property is named. It is not money to buy a farm, it is that particular farm. It is a basic rule that if the deceased disposed of an item making up a specific or special legacy, that legacy is adeemed and nothing is payable to the beneficiary in its place. The motives of the testator in disposing of the item are not relevant. Tough luck, Cuthbert!

(b) Augustus, Bill and Freda

The technical name for a "whom failing" provision is a destination-over. If, as in this case, the institute (Bill) survives the testator, he takes a full vested right and the property, both heritable and moveable, is his to dispose of as he wishes. Thus, he could sell any or all of it, give it away or dispose of it by will. If, as is possible in this case, he does none of these things, Freda may have at least some cause for optimism. Augustus' will may have provided its own rules but, if not, certain presumptions will come into play. If Freda was a conditional institute, any rights of succession to the property will have "flown off" when Bill inherited. If, on the other hand, Freda was a substitute she could still inherit, provided that Bill has not already alienated the property. Under s.8 of the Succession (Scotland) Act 2016, the second-named legatee is presumed to be a conditional institute; this can be defeated if the will states otherwise, or if the testator's intention can clearly be inferred.

Question 5

Stephen has recently died intestate in Scotland. He is survived by his wife, Mildred and daughter, Ella. His son, Tim, predeceased him, leaving two children, Jimmy and Ira, both of whom also survived their grandfather.

Stephen's estate after deduction of debts and funeral expenses consists of the following:

(i) His house at 22 Brewer Street, Aberdeen, owned jointly with Mildred and recently valued at £500,000;
(ii) His share of the contents of the house, a share which is worth £27,500;
(iii) His other moveable estate amounting to £77,000.

You are required to:
(a) Give a full explanation of the rules of intestate succession as they apply to this situation; and
(b) Prepare a scheme of division indicating, in accordance with those rules, how the estate will be divided between the members of the family.

(a) Explanation of intestate division

This is another classic question, some variation of which is often likely to come up in a succession examination. Requiring candidates to prepare an intestate scheme of division is an excellent way of simultaneously assessing knowledge, understanding and problem solving skills. Candidates would be well-advised to ensure that, if intestacy forms part of the assessable material, they are very well versed on the relevant rules and their application.

In answering this question, then, you should logically and carefully work through the various stages of intestate division, considering each relevant claim in turn. It is advisable to identify and explain each right, including what it is called, who is entitled to claim it, and what it entitles the claimant to receive. Do *not* simply look at the estate and try to decide who should get what from there; whilst that is the ultimate purpose of the exercise, it is far more liable to result in errors than a full consideration and application of the relevant law. Once you have fully explained what everyone is entitled to and why (and having checked that you have calculated everything correctly), you can then proceed to prepare the scheme of division itself.

So, explain that the first stage of intestate division (after debts and funeral expenses, which have already been deducted) is prior rights. There are three of these, all of which are claimable by a surviving spouse or civil partner under the Succession (Scotland) Act 1964. In this case, Stephen's surviving spouse Mildred may claim prior rights. Mildred is therefore entitled to claim Stephen's share of the dwellinghouse, a right worth £250,000 here, since she is already joint owner of the house. She can also claim Stephen's share of the furniture, a right worth £27,500 in this case (it might be worth mentioning that the maximum value is £29,000). Mildred can also claim a right to financial provision, in this case worth £50,000 since Stephen also left issue (again, it might be worth mentioning that if Stephen had left no issue, this right would be worth £89,000).

You should then explain that the second stage of intestate division is legal rights. These are claimed against the net moveable estate, which in this case is £27,000. The first legal right is Mildred's right to claim *jus relictae*, which entitles her to 1/3 of the net moveable estate, in this case £9,000. The second legal right is legitim, a collective claim whereby Stephen's issue can share 1/3 of the net moveable estate. In this case, the legitim claimants are Stephen's surviving daughter Ella, and his grandchildren Jimmy and Ira, who will represent Stephen's predeceasing son Tim. Since the claimants are in different degrees of relationship to the deceased, division will be *per stirpes*, with Ella taking half the legitim fund (£4,500), and Jimmy and Ira taking one quarter (£2,250) each.

The third and final stage is free estate (or dead's part), i.e. any estate, heritable and moveable, which remains undistributed at this point. Here, since there is no further heritable property, the free estate is all moveable, totalling £9,000. Under s.2 of the Succession (Scotland) Act 1964, this is claimable by the children (or their representatives) of the deceased, in this case Ella, Jimmy and Ira. Division is *per stirpes*, exactly as with the legitim fund; therefore Ella takes half (£4,500), and Jimmy and Ira take one quarter (£2,250) each.

Having performed these three stages of division, the estate is exhausted.

(b) Scheme of division

It is fair to say there is more than one way to prepare a scheme of division. For purposes of illustration, the scheme set out below follows the format already presented earlier in the book. This is a widely employed, and widely accepted, method.

	Heritable	**Moveable**
Estate		
Dwellinghouse	250,000	
Furniture		27,500
Other moveables		77,000
Balances	250,000	104,500
Deduct prior rights		
Dwellinghouse	(250,000)	
Furniture		(27,500)
Financial provision		(50,000)
Balances	Nil	27,000
Deduct legal rights		
Relict's part 1/3 NME		(9,000)
Legitim 1/3 NME		(9,000)

Balances	Nil	9,000
<u>Deduct free estate</u>		
To children		(9,000)
Balances	Nil	Nil

The final distribution would be:

Mildred

Prior Rights	£327,500
Relict's part	£9,000
TOTAL	£336,500

Ella

1/2 Legitim	£4,500
1/2 Free estate	£4,500
TOTAL	£9,000

Jimmy (representing Tim)

1/4 Legitim	£2,250
1/4 Free estate	£2,250
TOTAL	£4,500

Ira (representing Tim)

1/4 Legitim	£2,250
1/4 Free estate	£2,250
TOTAL	£4,500

APPENDIX 2: A TYPICAL TRUST DISPOSITION AND SETTLEMENT

The undernoted trust disposition and settlement might be considered fairly typical. The style of the document indicates that it has been drawn up in a traditional manner, perhaps some years ago. It does not, for example, contain the now common provision of postponing vesting for a period of 30 days after the testator's death. Space does not permit comment on every item, but attention is drawn to particular points by the comments in italics. The testing clause and signatures have been omitted; they would of course require to be completed in real life.

TRUST DISPOSITION AND SETTLEMENT OF JAMES BROWN

I, JAMES BROWN, Chartered Architect, Eleven Low Causeway, Inverdrearie, for the settlement of my means and estate after my death, do hereby ASSIGN, DISPONE and CONVEY to and in favour of my brother, NIGEL BROWN, Seventeen Anniesland Cross, Glasgow, my sister Mrs MAVIS BROWN or BYRD, Twenty Jute Street, Dundee and ALEXANDER FAIRSERVICE WYSE, Solicitor in Inverdrearie and to the acceptors and acceptor, survivors and survivor of them as trustees and trustee for the purposes aftermentioned (the trustees or trustee for the time being acting hereunder being hereinafter referred to as "my trustees") the whole means and estate, heritable and moveable, real and personal, wheresoever situated, which may belong to me or over which I shall have power of disposal at my death; And I appoint my trustees to be my executors; But these presents are granted in trust always for the following purposes: [*Yes, a bit verbose and slightly pompous, but reasonably clear. The testator is clearly setting up a trust which overlaps, but continues beyond, the period of executry. He prudently nominates a plurality of trustees; one might decline, another might predecease. The trustees are also expressly appointed as executors; this is common but not essential since testamentary trustees are statutorily executors, unless others are specifically appointed in the will.*]
FIRST For payment of my debts and funeral expenses and the expenses of administering the trust hereby created. [*This clause is not a requirement, but it is traditional.*]
SECOND I direct my trustees to make over the following specific legacies: (A) to my neighbour, Jack Spratt, Thirteen Low Causeway, Inverdrearie, my grand piano; [*Specific legacies are covered in Ch.5.*] (B) to my devoted Secretary, Miss Judith Panting, Eight Drumlie Street, Inverdrearie, provided she be in my employment at the date of my death, my grandfather clock; [*A classic example of a suspensive condition or a condition precedent. If the beneficiary fails to fulfil the condition of being in the testator's service at the time of his death, she acquires no right and the clock is part of the residue.*] (C) to my old friend, Magnus Merryman, Twelve Hope Street,

Aberdeen, whom failing to his wife, my gold hunter pocket watch. [*A clear example of a destination-over, with Magnus's wife being called as conditional institute; if both predecease the testator, the watch forms part of the residue.*]

THIRD I direct my trustees to pay, as soon as convenient after my death but without interest to the date of payment, the following general legacies: (A) to each of my nephews and nieces, Peter Brown, David Brown, Graeme Brown, Joan Brown and Cynthia Brown or Green who shall survive me, the sum of One Thousand Pounds; [*There will be no accretion if one or more of this class predeceases.*] (B) to the Kirk Session of the Martyrs' Church, Inverdrearie, the sum of Five Thousand Pounds to be applied towards the refurbishment of the Church steeple, declaring that a simple receipt signed by the Kirk Treasurer for the time being shall be sufficient discharge for my trustees. [*This provision could be somewhat dated. The church may have changed its name or united with another; perhaps the steeple was demolished five years ago! Unfortunately, no dispositive discretion is given to the trustees in the event of failure and there is a possibility that such a restricted provision could fail. The stipulation for a simple receipt to be an adequate discharge is sensible.*]

FOURTH I cancel the debt of Two Thousand pounds owing to me by Caleb Whyte, Forty Alexandra Street, Inverdrearie so far as the same, both capital and interest, is outstanding and unpaid at the date of my death. [*A nice gesture on the testator's part. Such a provision counts as a general legacy, should the matter of abatement arise.*]

FIFTH In the event of my wife Mrs Margaret Black or Brown surviving me, I direct my trustees to pay to her during all the days of her life (but subject as hereinafter provided) the free annual income of the residue of the trust estate, but that for her alimentary liferent use only [*Alimentary liferent is explained in Ch.5.*] and declaring that out of the said income my wife shall be bound, to the satisfaction of my trustees, suitably to maintain and educate such of our children as remain in family with her and are unable reasonably to provide for themselves, as to which my trustees shall be the sole judges; [*The late Mr Brown might not have won awards for political correctness!*] with power to my trustees, should they consider the said income insufficient for the suitable maintenance and education as aforesaid of my wife and our children to encroach upon capital as they may consider necessary for the said purposes but so that such payments shall not exceed one third of the capital of the residue of my estate; [*There can only be encroachment on capital to provide income for the liferenter if, as in this case, express authority is given.*] declaring however that in the event of my said wife entering into a further marriage after my death, the foregoing liferent provision in her favour shall forthwith cease and determine and the said residue of my estate shall be dealt with as hereinafter provided; [*The testator is ensuring that the family wealth is not reduced by the widow taking anything into a subsequent marriage. He is seeking to make adequate provision for his widow without drastically reducing what will eventually come to his children.*] And I direct that the provisions of the

Apportionment Act 1870 or of any other statute dealing with apportionment shall not apply to my estate. [*Mr Brown's solicitor would have put in this clause, disapplying the 1870 Act, to avoid the complicated calculations that would otherwise apply.*]
SIXTH In the event of my wife surviving me, then on her death or remarriage as hereinbefore provided, or, in the event of her predeceasing me, then on my death [*A classic example of fixing a certain day. If the wife dies before the testator, the liferent provision fails entirely. If she does survive, it is certain that the liferent will eventually end, either by her death or remarriage. This points to the fiars taking an immediate vested right on their father's death.*], I direct my trustees to pay and make over the rest, residue and remainder of my means and estate equally among such of my children Alexander, Roderick and Samantha as shall be then in life, together with any children then in life who may be born to my said wife and myself after the making of this will [*This is stated not only for the sake of clarity but to ensure that there is no danger of a subsequently born child invoking the conditio si testator and thus pushing the entire estate into intestacy.*], declaring that if any of my children shall predecease the date of division under this clause [*If his wife predeceases, the date of division is the testator's death. If his wife survives, the date of division is the end of the liferent. Children, in any event, take an immediate vested right on their father's death.*], leaving issue who shall survive the said date, such issue shall come in place of their parent and take *per stirpes* if more than one, the share original and accresced, which his, her or their parent would have taken if then alive. [*Any child who survives the testator takes a vested right at the date of his death; similarly the issue of any of Mr Brown's children who survive his death but die before the date of division inherit that vested right. However, if a child survives the testator, but dies before the date of division leaving no issue, that child's share would be subject to defeasance and would accresce to the shares applicable to the other children.*]
SEVENTH I provide and declare that in addition to the powers, privileges and immunities of gratuitous trustees by statute and under common law, my trustees shall have the fullest powers of and in regard to retention, realisation, investment, administration, management and division of my estate as if they were absolute beneficial owners thereof [*This would have been inserted to ensure that the trustees would not have to observe the somewhat irksome investment provisions of the Trustee Investment Act 1961, now abolished, so the provision is now redundant.*] with power to my trustees to appoint any one or more of their own number or any other person to act as factor or solicitor to the trust hereby created and to allow him, her or them the same professional remuneration in respect of such actings to which he, she or they would have been entitled if not a trustee or trustees; [*Mr Wyse, the solicitor, would have ensured that this part of the clause was included; otherwise, as a gratuitous trustee, he would be unable to make any charge for his professional services.]*
And I revoke all prior testamentary writings executed by me. *[Hopefully, any prior will has also been physically destroyed, either by the testator or by his solicitor, after express instructions.*] IN WITNESS WHEREOF. . .

INDEX